"BIG MACRAE"

The Rev. John Macrae
(1794-1876)

Memorials of a Notable Ministry

by

George N. M. Collins

*Professor of Church History
in the Free Church College, Edinburgh*

KNOX PRESS (EDINBURGH)
15 NORTH BANK STREET
EDINBURGH

1976

First published 1976

©

G. N. M. Collins

Printed by Lindsay & Co. Ltd., Edinburgh

CONTENTS

PREFACE

"The humblest Christian who is faithful to God may have the confidence that his influence for good will continue long after he has passed away from earth" — that is C. H. Irwin's comment on the dead man who came to life on being cast into the tomb of Elisha and coming into contact with the bones of the dead prophet.

The miracle has been repeated in countless instances as men have touched the bones of the Lord's prophets of former times through reading about them, and it is in the hope that the revitalising power of the Holy Spirit, Who made these prophets what they were, may operate anew through the story of John Macrae that I have compiled this short record of his ministry. For John Macrae was one of the greatest pulpiteers of the Highlands of Scotland in the 19th century, and his preaching was widely used by God for the conversion of sinners and the edification of saints. He paid little attention to style, and in the art of the homilist he called no man his master. His one aim in the pulpit was to preach the reconciliation of the Cross in language best suited to his hearers; and, as in the case of the Master Whose message he bore, "the common people heard him gladly."

I am deeply grateful to the Rev. Donald Gillies, M.A., the present minister of Lochs Free Church and Clerk of the Free Presbytery of Lewis, for his kind help in providing excerpts from the Presbytery records bearing on John Macrae's ministry, especially for those which bear on his attitude to the Church Union movement of his time.   G. N. M. Collins.

Facsimile of John Macrae's signature on the *Claim, Declaration and Protest* presented to Parliament in 1842.

Chapter One

INTRODUCING JOHN MACRAE

From my schoolboy days John Macrae had a peculiar fascination for me. The grave had closed over all that was mortal of him some forty years before I first heard mention of his name, but in an odd kind of way he seemed strangely contemporary. This may have been, in part at least, because we had no minister of our own, and the good elder who, as we said, "kept the door open" used often to regale us with "notes" from the famous divines of the past. And none of these, with the possible exception of Thomas Boston himself, stood in higher favour with him than John Macrae. There may have been an element of clannishness in his choice, for our missionary-elder was a Macrae himself, although not of any known kinship to his hero. But Duncan Macrae had a fondness for marrowy doctrine and picturesque presentation. And John Macrae's sermons were both arrestive to the mind and meaty to the soul. Duncan Macrae never presumed to preach, in the formal sense of the word, but he was well read in the Gaelic religious literature that was available and we received the benefit of his diligence. Along with this he made an annual circuit of neighbouring communion gatherings where he and like-minded brethren would often call to mind the days of old and rehearse choice sayings gleaned from the great

Gospel preachers of palmier days. And thus it came about that when he returned from his annual pilgrimages, he came with a fresh stock of spiritual gleanings with which he loved to regale us from the reader's desk. It was evident to all that he enjoyed the purveying of them — especially those that he could link with the honoured name of John Macrae, and we — yes, even the juniors — enjoyed them too. For Duncan Macrae had a fine gift of description, and the stories of his clansman lost nothing in the telling. Very vividly do I still remember his relation of John Macrae's parable of the maggot making its way to Stornoway, and its encounter with the traveller who questioned it.

"You look tired, little maggot," said the traveller, "where are you going?"

"I'm on my way to Stornoway," replied the maggot. "I have heard that there is a hogshead of sugar there and I want to get to it."

"But the way is long, little maggot, and you are weak and in danger of being trodden underfoot."

"I know," quoth the indomitable maggot, "I know that the way is long, and that I am feeble and in danger of being crushed underfoot. But if I once get my head into that hogshead of sugar in Stornoway I shall remember no more my own feebleness nor the length and dangers of the way."

We thought the story was left incomplete; but our seniors smiled knowingly. They understood. It was a homely allegory, a pictorial commentary on Paul's brave comparison: *"For I reckon that the sufferings of this present time are not worthy to be*

8

compared with the glory which shall be revealed in us" (Rom. 8: 18).

Needless to say, that quotation from John Macrae belonged to his ministry in Lewis where Stornoway was the centre of commercial life for the villages round about.

There was one fragment of John Macrae's teaching that proved to one hearer, at least, a veritable "word in season." It was communion time, and one of the preachers for the occasion was the Rev. George Mackay, of Fearn. Mr Mackay had been Free Church minister in Stornoway at a time when "Big Macrae" anecdotes bulked large in the spiritual currency of the Island of Lewis, and he had amassed a considerable store of them. On the occasion to which I refer he was dispensing the sacrament of the Lord's Supper with heart-winning tenderness and sympathetic understanding when he called John Macrae to his aid. He had been speaking words of comfort and encouragement to those at the table who might be downcast and disconsolate because the first ardent glow of Christian experience appeared to have spent itself. Drawing upon a remarkably accurate memory, he reproduced the gist of a communion table address once given by Mr Macrae. It was based on the words of Mary Magdalene: *"They have taken away my Lord, and I know not where they have laid Him"* (John 20: 13).

"Here," said the preacher, "we have the mourning of a gracious soul for an absent Lord, and methinks I hear one in this gathering saying, 'I used to find the Lord in the preaching of the Word, but I do not find Him there now. *They*

9

have taken away my Lord, and I know not where they have laid Him.'

"But another says, 'My condition is worse than that, for I used to find the Lord, not only in the preaching but also in the reading of the Word, and I do not find Him there now. *They have taken away my Lord, and I know not where they have laid Him.'*

"But another says, 'My condition is even worse than that, for I used to find Him not only in the preaching and in the hearing of the Word, but also in private prayer, and I do not find Him in any of these three places now. *They have taken away my Lord, and I know not where they have laid Him.'*

"But I hear yet another saying, 'My condition is the worst of all; for I used to find Him not only in those places, but also in the fellowship of His people, and I do not find Him there now. *They have taken away my Lord, and I know not where they have laid Him.'*

"Poor soul, if that is your complaint, I will tell you three places out of which they cannot take away your Lord. (1) They can never take Him away out of the everlasting Covenant of Grace. (2) They can never take Him away out of the free offer of the Gospel. And (3) they can never take Him away out of the longing which has been awakened by grace in your own soul."

One hearer, not at the table that day, listened with eagerness and wonder to the closing words of this unusual address. Was it possible that the first stirrings of a longing for Christ which he now sensed in his soul were really the effect of saving grace? More amazing still, could it really be that

that longing for Christ signified that he already possessed Him?

No, he was not at the Lord's Table that day, but Mr Macrae's words did much to open the way for him when, in due time, he did come.

The years passed and, now a final year student in theology, I was in Greenock to preach in the vacant Free Gaelic Church there. A call to the pastorate ensued, and some weeks later I was ordained and inducted to the charge, the seventh in succession from "Big Macrae."

It was disappointing to learn that his pulpit had been replaced during the ministry of the Rev. Murdoch Macaskill. But when, after the prayer meeting on the following Wednesday evening I asked one of the senior office-bearers if he knew what had happened to it, he echoed my query: "What has happened to it? Why you were preaching in it this very night."

And it is still there, in the larger hall of the Free Gaelic Church.

A visit to the Gabriel Wood Mariners' Asylum shortly thereafter brought me another reminder of John Macrae. One of the old seamen beckoned to me as I was about to leave the building, and asked me if I were the new minister of the Free Gaelic Church. When I replied that I was, another question followed.

"Did you ever hear of the Rev. John Macrae?"

I replied, with fresh interest, that I had.

"It was he," said he, "who baptised me."

It was my only living link with the ministry of "Big Macrae" in Greenock.

I left Greenock in 1938 to become minister of Free St Columba's Church in Edinburgh. And still I seemed to be following in the footsteps of John Macrae, for soon thereafter it was my privilege to welcome one of his granddaughters and her family into the fellowship of the congregation. And it is as a result of that contact that I have been able to draw upon his notes in his interleaved study-Bible, and upon a collection of his letters, all in his handwriting, as clear and legible as it was a century ago, and to use the material so gleaned for the compilation of this book.

Yes, I *must* write something about him. I owe it to him, and to others. And the appropriate time seems to be *now*, in the centennial year of his death.

Chapter Two

EARLY LIFE AND CONVERSION

John Macrae was born (according to his biographer, Nicol Nicolson) at Achadh-nan-Gart, in Kintail, in 1794. He came of a large family, six of whom died in early life. Of the remaining six, John was the youngest. He was still a child when his parents removed to Ardelve in Lochalsh. He was of the true Macrae stock, for both his parents belonged to the clan. For nineteen years the Macrae family remained in Ardelve, and then removed to Morvich, in Kintail. Within a year the father died, and shortly thereafter John and one of his brothers rented a sheep-farm at Immir, at the south end of Lochcarron.

There was still no trace of saving grace in John Macrae, nor any prospect that he would yet turn from shepherding in his own interests to taking the oversight of Christ's flock as the servant of the Good Shepherd. He was an honest and industrious man, but his affections were set on nothing higher than the things of the earth. When he first attracted the attention of the godly men of his time it was certainly not by any promise of a growing interest in the Gospel; rather the reverse. The story has often been told how the Rev. Lachlan Mackenzie of Lochcarron — the widely famed "Mr Lachlan" — and his friend, the Rev. John Kennedy of Redcastle, once heard him directing his sheepdogs in a voice that registered wrath of high temperature, and in words that fell offensively on the ears of his godly auditors.

"What a powerful, rough voice that young man has!" exclaimed Mr Kennedy. But Mr Mackenzie was a bit of a seer. "True," he replied, "and I am well accustomed to that voice. But I seem to hear a meek and quiet voice behind those rugged sounds. I do not expect to see it, John, but you may live to see the time when your eyes and ears can testify that no one, in his day, can surpass that young man in proclaiming from the pulpit the grace of God in Christ Jesus to perishing sinners."

And so in due course it happened; but the time was not yet. The Clan Macrae comprised the "Fair Macraes" and the "Black Macraes", and when a friend once asked John in his early days to which division he belonged, he replied, "To the Fair Macraes."

"Then," responded his friend, "God have mercy on the Black ones!"

John's physical strength was proverbial, and many of his exploits have been recorded. Returning from the Inverness market on one occasion, he and another farmer rested and refreshed themselves awhile at an inn. His companion urged an early departure so as to get home in daylight, but John stayed on, letting his timid companion set out alone. But "two are better than one", and for lack of a sturdy second the hapless traveller was overcome by three thieves who stole the money that he had made at the market. In the hope of increasing their hoard they still prowled for victims, and John Macrae was the next to come along. All three rushed at him demanding his money or his life. Karate was not heard of in the Highlands in those days, but John Macrae had a system of his own! He threw a piece of money on the ground, and when one of the footpads stooped to pick it up, something hit him that made him ineffective for the rest of the encounter! The second prowler also had a swift despatch. The third fell into a clutch that made him cry for mercy.

Among the plunder found in the possession of the thieves John recognised the wallet of his companion who had gone ahead of him, and he took charge of it. Proceeding on his way he overtook his disconsolate friend at Garve Inn, and quickly changed the robbed man's sorrow into joy by throwing his lost property on the table in front of him — the evidence that Macrae's strong arm had won the day.

During his time as parish teacher in Uig, Mr Macrae once visited Stornoway to stock up with provisions for the winter. One of his purchases was a barrel of salt herring, a popular standby for winter fare in those days.

"I hear," said the fish curer, "that you are the Samson of our island. The barrel of herring is yours for nothing if you can carry it away in your arms."

The salesman's challenge cost him more than he had bargained for. A second barrel of herring stood by the one John Macrae had wanted to purchase. Encircling each barrel with a powerful arm he lifted them and made off with them, to the amazement and delight of his challenger.

But it was not by such feats of physical

strength that John Macrae was to make his name in the Highlands of Scotland, but by exploits that can be performed only in the strength that is perfected in weakness.

John Macrae's son-in-law, the Rev. Donald Macmaster, who wrote the biographical sketch of him which appears in *Disruption Worthies of the Highlands*, traces the beginnings of the spiritual change in him to the influence of a sister whose "living piety (writes Mr Macmaster) made him uneasy about himself, and convinced him that there is a reality in religion to which he was a stranger."

The Rev. Nicol Nicolson mentions another helpful influence. In those days, a noted evangelist used to itinerate large areas of the Highlands. Finlay Munro — for that was his name — owed little to the schools, and the schools could have made little of him in any case, for he was rather weak-minded. But Finlay was one of the "weak things of the world" that God chose, "to confound the things that are mighty." With a heart aflame with the love of Christ, and a burning zeal for the conversion of souls, Finlay went his unplanned rounds, commending Christ in word and walk, and proclaiming God's gracious provision for the salvation of the transgressor.

At the time of John Macrae's encounter with him, a road was being constructed over the risky Mam Ratagan in Wester Ross, and John Macrae was there to superintend the undertaking. One day, when the men were resting for their midday snack, Finlay appeared on the scene and was cordially invited to join in. Gratefully, he did so, but not until he had acknowledged God's hand in providing for them and given thanks for his portion. And as John Macrae listened to the good man's words he was deeply impressed. God seemed awesomely near. Yet it seemed as if these better moods were as "a morning cloud, and as the early dew" that "passeth away."

John Macrae's ultimate apprehension for Christ came through the instrumentality of the famous minister of Ferintosh, Dr John MacDonald, "the Apostle of the North."

Whether or not John Macrae knew that Dr MacDonald was to be preaching in the open air at Port-na-cloiche that day, by all accounts it was not from any desire to hear him that he placed himself within reach of the preacher's voice. Indeed, it was strongly suspected that his shepherding activities on that occasion were prompted by the desire to annoy the preacher and distract his hearers. But what happened was that he came within range of the preacher's artillery and sustained a grievous wound. Dr MacDonald's text was: *"Go forth: O ye daughters of Zion, and behold King Solomon with the crown wherewith his mother crowned him in the day of his espousals, and in the day of the gladness of his heart"* (Song of Solomon 3: 11). John Macrae was given a glimpse of the king "greater than Solomon", and the vision filled him with the profoundest disquiet. With Isaiah he could have cried, *"Woe is me! for I am undone; because I am a man of unclean lips, and I dwell in the midst of a people of unclean lips; for mine eyes have seen the King, the Lord of hosts"* (Isaiah 6: 5). His convictions of sin were deep and

17

distressing. The man of proverbial strength became a shorn Samson — "weak as other men"; indeed, his very life seemed to be in danger. His loud cries for pardon seemed to storm the battlements of heaven in vain. Had he, in his folly, passed --

> . . . the line unseen
>   that crosses every path,
> The hidden boundary between
>   God's patience and His wrath?

The communion seasons at Ferintosh, on the other side of the county, were great occasions in those days, and attracted multitudes of worshippers from round about. With flickering hope John Macrae decided to join them. God had used Dr MacDonald to cast him down; perhaps the same hand might be used to raise him up. He would put the matter to the test.

It was not until the Sabbath evening of the communion season that deliverance came, however, and it came, not by means of John MacDonald, but through the spirit-filled message with which Dr Angus MacIntosh, of Tain, brought that "solemn, holy day" to a close. In an appeal to the unconverted, such as was customary on the evening of the Communion Sabbath, he pointed them to Him Who came "to call not the righteous but sinners to repentance."

John Macrae returned home in the comfort of saving grace. For him thenceforward there was to be:

> None other Lamb, none other Name,
> None other Hope in heaven or earth or sea,
> None other hiding-place from guilt and
>   shame,
> None beside Thee.

The change wrought in him soon became evident to those who knew him best. One of these, a relative, a powerfully built man like John himself — was hard to convince. "I will not believe," he protested, "until I see him, and put the matter to the proof."

His way of putting the matter to the proof was rather novel. He had often wrestled with his kinsman in the past, but had never worsted him. Could the change in him be traced to a physical source? Was he, in fact, going soft? When he tested his theory in his next encounter with John its wrongness was fully demonstrated! John threw him with the same measure of ease as on past occasions! The explanation of the change must lie elsewhere. With sharpened curiosity he went to hear Macrae at his next meeting, and came away deeply impressed if not greatly enlightened by what he heard. "There is something in religion," he said, "that people do not always understand when it could throw Big John Macrae!"

It was soon made evident to John Macrae that God had new plans for his life. The call to the ministry of the Word now came to him with an insistence that made his duty clear, and we next find him enrolled in Aberdeen University as a student in arts. He had been given a solid, if restricted, education in earlier life, and this became a firm foundation for the higher studies that marked the way to his chosen vocation. Mathematics especially appealed to him and he attained a proved proficiency in the subject. For his theological course he removed to Edinburgh where he revelled in the teaching of Dr Thomas Chalmers, who was Professor of Theology in the

University there at the time. Chalmers had a great fascination for him, and it may be that, unconsciously, the student modelled himself upon his famous master. For Dr Robert S. Candlish once described John Macrae as "the Chalmers of the Highlands," and Dr Alexander Beith, of Stirling, bracketed Chalmers and Macrae together as the "two most glorious preachers" of the day in Scotland. Chalmers would not have been displeased by the comparison, for he held his former student in the highest esteem and, meeting him in Edinburgh on one occasion, after Macrae had begun to make his name as a preacher and churchman, he pronounced the Aaronic benediction over him!

But we have not yet reached that point in his story.

Divine acknowledgment of Mr Macrae's labours began early. The district of Arnisdale, in Inverness-shire, yielded him his first fruits in the Gospel, for in his early studies he gave part-time teaching service there. During that preparatory period he began to hold meetings for the older people on the Lord's day, and to conduct prayer meetings through the week. Almost from the beginning, his word was "in demonstration of the Spirit and of power." The Rev. Donald Macmaster records that "a work of grace began in the district as striking and as satisfactory as he at all saw in his after career."

It was the first fruits of the abundant harvest that was soon to follow.

Chapter Three

THE CALL TO SERVICE

Before being ordained to the ministry John Macrae served for some time as teacher in the parish of Uig, in Lewis. There he became associated with the Rev. Alexander Macleod, through whose faithful ministry, rich, spiritual blessing came to the parish. And it would be difficult to imagine a parish that stood in greater need of such a visitation of grace. When Alexander Macleod went there in 1824 there were over 800 communicant members in the congregation, few of whom bore any traces of spiritual life. Pagan worship was still practised among them, and Sabbath trading was part of their normal life.

Appalled at the spiritual condition of his flock, Macleod laboured to bring home to them the danger of their plight, and decided not to dispense the sacrament of the Lord's Supper to them until they had come to an awareness of the true significance of the ordinance, and to a sense of their own unfitness to receive it. A year passed without communion services, but when Mr Macleod decided to withhold the sacrament for a second year a storm of opposition broke out in the island. The Stornoway minister sent a messenger to Uig with a bag of communion tokens for the communicants who were to be denied the opportunity of communicating in their

21

home parish. But the communion tokens were never delivered. The Rev. Alexander Macleod consulted with John Macrae and Francis MacBean in the matter, and Macrae proposed that he should intercept the messenger and deprive him of the tokens. But Alexander Macleod would not hear of it. John Macrae was reminded that such an action might have unhappy consequences for him; he was the parish teacher and the Presbytery had authority over him. Francis MacBean, as a seceder and Inspector of the Gaelic schools, was under no such restriction, however, and he it was who carried out the plan which his companion had suggested. The bearer of the tokens was relieved of his trust.

The sequel had an amusing side to it. The Presbytery took action against Mr Macleod for withholding the sacrament of the Lord's Supper from the people of Uig, and tried to coerce him into compliance with their desire. All the ministers of the Presbytery, they reminded him, were opposed to him. To this, Mr Macleod replied, undauntedly, that he cared little for such opposition; the "Great Minister" (meaning Jesus Christ, the Head of the Church) was on his side.

The Rev. Alexander Simpson, of Lochs, who was an outsize of a man, took Macleod's words as a reference to himself and was gratified by the compliment! "That is right, Macleod," he bellowed, "I *am* on your side, and we shall defy them."

And that was the end of the Presbyterial action against Mr Macleod!

In the following year the first celebration of

the Lord's Supper in Mr Macleod's ministry in Uig took place. There were only six communicants, but there was a great congregation. Soon the parish was in the throes of revival, and vast crowds of people gathered to the meetings. For five years the revival fires burned brightly, and their glow was seen and felt all over the island. Indeed, there might be good cause for saying that the enlivening effect of those memorable years is still being felt in Lewis. Excellency of speech contributed little to the movement; John Macrae said of Mr Macleod's preaching that it was "a striking instance of how the foolishness of preaching was made effective by God." But he testified that the finest moral spectacle he had ever witnessed during his whole career was that of the congregation of Uig under the pastorate of the Rev. Alexander Macleod.

It was a wonderful and fitting introduction to the evangelical ministry on which he was soon to enter.

Principal John Macleod in his *Bypaths of Highland Church History*, referring to the partnership between John Macrae and Francis MacBean in Lewis, records that they took leading parts in the first "Question Meeting" to be held in the island — Mr MacBean "opening the question," and Mr Macrae closing the discussion. This was at Stornoway communion in 1825 or 1826.

Chapter Four

THE PREACHER AND DEPUTY

It was to the Presbytery of Chanonry that the honour fell of licensing Mr Macrae as a preacher of the Word. That was in 1830, and for a time thereafter he assisted the Rev. James Russell, minister of Gairloch. The discerning people of Wester Ross took him at once to their hearts and never failed to rally to him when, in after years, he preached in the neighbourhood. But it was Lewis that first gave him a pastorate of his own, and in 1833 he was ordained and inducted as minister of the large congregation of Cross. The Rev. Finlay Cook had served in the Parliamentary Church there before him, so that it was not into virgin soil that Mr Macrae thrust his plough-share. But much remained to be done, and his wide and wild parish, and the many wild people still in it, taxed the endurance of the young pastor.

A wastrel in the community tried to frighten him on one occasion. Wrapping himself in a cow-hide, with the horns of the cow sticking out from his head, he waylaid the minister on a dark and dreary road between the townships, at one moment appearing in front of him in the dim light, and then stealing into the shadows to appear again behind him or beside him. Several times, the minister advised him to desist from his folly, but he still continued to play the devil.

The ultimate warning was issued: "If you are a

devil incarnate, you will feel the weight of my arm if you do not go away at once."

But still the "devil" refused to be dismissed.

"Take that then," said Mr Macrae, swinging a heavy blow at his tormentor, "and betake yourself to God, asking Him to have mercy on your soul."

The worth of Peter's advice, "Resist the devil and he will flee from you," was fully demonstrated! The stunned "devil" slunk away into the shadows, horns, hide and all, completely discomfited. His minister had taught him a lesson that night that had lasting effects.

Some time afterwards he made his way to the manse to identify himself as the man who had tried to scare the minister, and to add, "I trust that was the last act that I shall ever perform in the service of the devil."

It is easy to believe that it wasn't, for there is no perfection in this life. But the end of the story was that the man who had tried to scare Mr Macrae out of the parish subsequently became a convert to Christ, through his ministry, and an office-bearer in the congregation.

Mr Macrae stayed on in Ness to outwit the real devil in many other encounters, and, as God's workman, to build up a strong and devoted congregation in a needy area. The measure of his success came to light in the fact that the interest in evangelical religion, which he was at pains to foster, continued to widen and deepen until, at the Disruption in 1843, the Established Church of the parish practically emptied itself into the Free Church of Scotland.

The congregation that, in 1839, reclaimed John Macrae for the Highland mainland was that of

Knockbain in Easter Ross, and it was there that he reached the zenith of his powers and became known as "Macrath Mor" ("Big Macrae") — not only because of his massive physical build but principally because of his powerful preaching, and his commanding influence in the Church, particularly in the Highland area.

In Easter Ross Mr Macrae found himself among like-minded ministerial neighbours. Dr John MacDonald, whose ministry had been so blessed to him in earlier years, was still at Ferintosh. John Kennedy, the father of the more famous Dr John Kennedy of Dingwall, was minister of Killearnan. In Resolis, the Rev. Donald Sage, who in 1822 had exchanged the Gaelic Chapel in Aberdeen for this rural pastorate, was prosecuting an edifying ministry and diligently compiling his famous *Memorabilia Domestica*. Cromarty had the inestimable privilege of being under the pastoral care of Alexander Stewart, whose convert, Hugh Miller the geologist, became the journalist of the Evangelical party in the Church of Scotland who formed the Free Church of Scotland in 1843. There were others of lesser stature but like faith; so that by his removal to Knockbain the lines fell to John Macrae in pleasant places. Yet his life in Easter Ross was not one of ease and tranquillity, for the Church in Scotland was in the grip of a controversy which was soon to cause separation between Church and State, and create deep division in the Church itself.

The story of those stirring years has often been told. The Church of the Reformers and the Covenanting martyrs had largely lost the spirit of former times when she had deemed Christ's crown and covenant to be a cause deserving the sacrifice even of life itself for its maintenance. Pliable clerics had sold out to grasping politicians. The Spiritual Independence of the Church was being taken from her. The crown of Christ as Head of the Church was being transferred to Caesar, and His Kingdom was being degraded into a mere department of State. Patrons were intruding ill-chosen nominees upon protesting congregations and the law-courts were legalising their misdeeds. The last scene in the tragic conflict was being set. An appeal, stating the grievances of a people deprived of their spiritual rights, was being prepared for presentation to Parliament. Everything depended upon the outcome of this final demand for justice. A now-resurgent Evangelical party was determined to maintain the rightful autonomy of the Church even if it meant the surrender of State support and all the advantages that were entailed therein. There was to be no surrender.

The rallying of the people to the support of the Church required the utmost exertions of the protesting ministers, and no one gave himself more enthusiastically to the work than did John Macrae of Knockbain. Dr Chalmers selected him as a deputy to visit the Highlands and Islands and acquaint the people with the matters at issue. By now he was well known all over the North as a preacher of outstanding prominence, and wherever he appeared he was assured of a large audience. His popularity was the dread of the opposing party, and they did their utmost to discredit him and bring him into disrepute. But the man who would parry Macrae's blade must be deft with his weapon. At a meeting in Lochcarron, where his companion, the Rev. James MacDonald, of Urray, was explaining the existing ecclesiastical situation to the audience, an Established Church minister who was present stood up and interrupted the speaker with the scornful remark, "You need not be so conceited, James, telling *us* the causes of the Disruption. Well do I remember when I used to teach you in your father's house."

It was John Macrae who replied, and the reply was not to the interrupter's liking. Rising again in the audience, he shouted, "I knew you right well, too, when you used to be hunting foxes in these wilds above us."

"Quite right," retorted Macrae, "but I find I did not extirpate them all when I see *you* still here." The valiant interrupter abandoned the meeting!

But though the weapon of repartee was always ready to Mr Macrae's hand it was used only when needed. His addresses were not the irresponsible productions of the demagogue, but the well-reasoned and edifying utterances of a discerner of the times. His work in this connection, was referred to by Dr Robert Elder, of Rothesay, in the following tribute extracted from a memorial sermon preached shortly after Mr Macrae's death. "Of his great and valuable services to our beloved Free Church I cannot here speak particularly. At the Disruption period he was, as I can testify from personal recollection and experience, a great power in the north and in the west, in expounding and defending, as few men could, the glorious prerogatives of the Lord Jesus Christ, as sole King and Head of His Church, the independence of Christ's Church with reference to civil authority, and her sole subjection to Him and His laws in spiritual things; and also in vindicating the blood-bought privileges of His Church and people. Perhaps there was no minister who exerted a more commanding influence in leading the minds of the people to clear views of duty during that eventful crisis."

Yet it was not, after all, as the spokesman of the aggrieved Church that John Macrae was best remembered in Knockbain, but as the ambassador of Christ commissioned to beseech men in Christ's stead that they be reconciled to God. It was in the exercise of that commission that his true greatness came to light.

A native of those parts wrote of him — particularly with reference to his Knockbain ministry — "In the pulpit, Mr Macrae's appearance was picturesque. His voice was of great compass. He possessed a powerful mind, which largely enabled him to overcome early disadvantages. In the Highlands, and especially in the western parts, his popularity as a herald of the Cross rose to an eminence rarely equalled. His statement of doctrine was lucid, and his application of it to the heart and conscience strikingly powerful. The Lord's people welcomed him, and benefited by his preaching, while his animated and stirring addresses arrested the careless and roused the slumbering, and were the means, in the hand of the Holy Spirit, of conviction and conversion."*

*Religious Life in Ross. Noble; p 281.

There were times when Mr Macrae's preaching disclosed a knowledge of events in the lives of his hearers that could not possibly have come to him by the usual media of communication. Hector Jack, of Strathconon, for instance, rose early one Sabbath morning to go to Knockbain. As he listened to the preacher, he was astonished to hear his own experiences so accurately described, but he could not really believe that the message had a special reference to him. At this point, Mr Macrae broke in upon his line of thought by exclaiming, "Young man, you are wondering if I am referring to somebody else, but I am not; I am referring to *you* who were so anxious last night lest you should sleep in that you divested yourself of only part of your clothes when you went to bed." This was exactly what Hector Jack had done, but still he thought the description might apply to somebody else in the congregation.

Once more, Mr Macrae raised his voice to a yet higher pitch, and said with great emphasis, "You are still thinking young man, that I may be referring to someone else in this gathering. To put it beyond all doubt for you, I am referring to *you,* who, in addition to what I have already said, prayed beneath the willow-bush in your back-garden before you left for Knockbain this morning."

The identification needed no further elaboration. The visitor gratefully accepted the comfort of the preacher's message, and, with overflowing joy, gave thanks to God who, by His servant, had spoken to him the very message that he so urgently needed and desired.

Mr Macrae's ministry of ten years in Knockbain made a deep and abiding impression upon Easter Ross — an area long used to great ministries; and, when he left, Hugh Miller spoke of him as "the last of the Ross-shire ministers." This obviously was the estimate of a strong partisan, and not many would have accepted it; for Ross-shire still retained a remarkable ministerial succession. But there was something quite unique about the preaching of John Macrae. What Christmas Evans was in the Welsh pulpit, John Macrae was in the Scottish. There were the same powers of imagination; the same gift of vivid description; the same lightning-flashes of spiritual illumination; the same deep insights into the things of the Spirit of God; withal the same strain of Celtic mysticism, and the same power of appeal as they laboured to commend to lost sinners the Saviour who came "to seek and to save that which is lost."

The shafts that wounded the convicted sinner, and the oil that healed him were both the provision of the Holy Spirit who alone makes the Word effectual unto salvation, and many could sing with Dora Greenwell:

Since He's taken this cold, dark heart of mine,
And has pierced it through and through,
He's taught me to grieve both for things that I
*   did,*
And for things that I didn't do.
He has showed me the Cross where He died for
*   me,*
And I'll end where I begin,
With an eye that looks to my Saviour,
And a heart that mourns for its sin.

31

Chapter Five

TIMES OF REFRESHING

John Macrae's one experience of a south-country ministry was in Greenock, and even there he dwelt among his own people. The expanding industries of the Clydeside had attracted vast numbers of men from the Highlands, and many of these had settled in the lower reaches of the estuary—particularly in Dumbarton, Port Glasgow and Greenock. For the Highland communities on the south bank of the estuary the Church of Scotland had made provision by setting up the Gaelic Chapel in Greenock. From the beginning, the note of the evangel sounded clearly in this sanctuary, and a well-instructed and discerning congregation filled its pews at almost every service. The Rev. Angus MacBean, a native of Moy, Inverness-shire, was minister there at the time of the Disruption, and almost the entire congregation came out of the Establishment with him and formed the Free Gaelic Church. Apart from its numerical strength, the beginnings of the new congregation were not auspicious. For lack of more suitable accommodation they had to worship, for some months, in a large tent pitched in the Duncan Street burying ground. Later they obtained more comfortable quarters in the old West Church, but by September 1844 they were in their new church in Jamaica Street. It was a plain building, but excellently designed for the needs of a large and growing congregation, and built to last. Angus MacBean's ministry there was not to be of long duration. He died in 1845.

This was the congregation, then, that in 1849 successfully called John Macrae to be their pastor. Greenock welcomed him with warmth and pride, for his fame had gone throughout the whole of Gaeldom. The new church was soon packed to the doors, and became a veritable house of God and gate of heaven to many. The spiritual blessing which had so deeply marked his earlier ministries in Lewis and Ross-shire was not less discernible in his Clydeside labours. But the excessive toils of the Disruption period had taken a toll which even his massive strength could ill afford. His health began to cause anxiety, and when in 1857 the congregation of Lochs, in Lewis, addressed a call to him it seemed to him that the leading of Divine Providence was in the event. The purer air of the Western Isles might restore him some of his lost energy and give him an extension of ministry. To the grief of an attached people, he accepted the call from Lochs.

The pastorate to which Mr Macrae removed from Greenock, did indeed provide him with a purer air, but, as well, it presented him with a programme of work that cancelled out the benefit. For Lochs in those days covered a wide area which in later times was broken up into the three congregational territories of Crossbost, Balallan and Park. The congregation numbered around 5,000 people. Roads were few and rough, so that sea transport was more practicable than that of horse-drawn vehicles. It was with this in view that the people of Snizort, in the Isle of

Skye—where Mr Macrae was as greatly loved as in Lewis itself—presented him with a serviceable yacht.

This gift originated in the kind thought of the Rev. Roderick Macleod, of Snizort, the "Apostle of Skye," whose evangelical preaching, once he had been delivered from the prevailing Moderatism, brought blessing to the island throughout its borders. Mr Macleod himself sailed the boat to Lewis so as to have the satisfaction of handing her over to his friend, the minister of Lochs. As well as being of great use to him in the pastoral oversight of his people, the yacht was also called into requisition at communion times when the manse became overcrowded by visitors who had come from distant parishes. Several people could be accommodated on her as she lay at anchor nearby.

Norman C. Macfarlane tells how he came to know the little ship intimately in his youth. Mr Macrae had gifted the yacht to Norman's uncle when he left Lochs for Carloway. "How often as a boy," recalls Mr Macfarlane, "I clambered on to the deck of *The Wild Duck!*" It was a prized contact with the minister who had made such early, and lasting impressions upon him.

Mr Macrae's popularity in Skye had been established by a strange incident which may be related here. When he had gone to Greenock from Knockbain his Lewis following had learned of the event with deep regret. While he was in the North there was always some hope of hearing him, but now he seemed to have put himself completely beyond their bounds. But when the news leaked through to Lewis that "Big Macrae" was to be at a communion in Skye two of his disciples in Lewis, Donald and Angus Morrison, decided that they would be there too. Greenock they could not reach, but Skye presented no such problem of remoteness.

But when they got to Skye, disappointment awaited them. Yes, John Macrae was there, but so too was George Macleod of Lochbroom, and Macleod was a prime favourite, whereas John Macrae was not yet so well known. Macleod, therefore, was given the principal services while Macrae was left with the sparsely attended English ones. The visitors from Lewis had very little English and their disappointment was extreme. They had come all that distance to hear their favourite preacher, only to be tantalised by hearing him in a language they could not well follow. They told Rev. Roderick Macleod of their plight and begged that Mr Macrae be given a Gaelic service. Mr Macleod consented, and by so doing incurred the displeasure of the Skye elders present, who could never get enough of their favourite, George Macleod. But the service went on, and John Macrae was at his best. The Skyemen became enraptured, and afterwards thanked the Lewis visitors who had been the means of providing for them such a veritable feast of fat things. Thereafter Mr Macrae's place in the Isle of Skye was secure, and he was much in demand at communion gatherings. When, therefore, he returned from Greenock to the Western Isles, the gift of the yacht expressed their delight that he was back, and their desire that he should visit them frequently in his apostolic journeyings and preach to them the unsearchable riches of Christ.

Macrae was well-suited to an island parish. The sea was in his blood, and he was used to it in all its changing moods. The story of an exploit in his earlier Lewis ministry had established his reputation as a seaman. The Rev. N. C. Macfarlane tells it in graphic detail. "He and some Ness folk," writes Macfarlane, "had gone to Steinish for Stornoway by boat. On the return passage a great storm arose. After rounding Tolsta Head, where the wild Atlantic leaps and roars against the sea gates of the Lews, the oarsmen, who had toiled until they were bone-weary, were about to give up. The rage of the mounting waves crushed them. Macrae's earlier sailoring came now to his aid with compound interest. He rallied the men and threatened them. It was his threatening that roused them. He said that he would apply the tiller to the first man who ceased rowing. He was not now their minister but their skipper.

Their experience that day enhanced Mr Macrae in their eyes, and his people feared him with a growing fear."

To have a minister who was not only a powerful preacher but also an experienced and intrepid seaman was something to be proud of.

But even the seas which break upon the Western Isles are not always stormy, and Mr Macrae loved them in their softer moods. "I was away yesterday," he writes to a friend, "preaching ten miles away from here, and returned last night about seven, more refreshed than fatigued by the exertion. We had a fine sail up and down a loch—very narrow for the most part, with low hills and hamlets on each side."

The measure of "exertion" that Lewis services required in those days may be judged by a reference to a communion in Barvas that Mr Macrae makes in a letter to his son-in-law. Rev. Donald Macmaster, of Back Free Church. "The day was cold," he writes, "but the services short. Began at quarter to 12, and finished at quarter past four, with six tables. There is concise work for you!" Would even Lewis regard that as an example in conciseness today?

Mr Macrae had been preceded in Lochs by the Rev. Robert Finlayson, a Caithness man, who had returned to the vicinity of his birth-place when he accepted a call to Helmsdale in 1856. A winsome preacher with a rare gift of expression Mr Finlayson had given twenty-five years of prayerful toil to Lochs with God-glorifying results. And now John Macrae had come to take up the work that Robert Finlayson had relinquished. A more promising successor could hardly be imagined. "Mr Finlayson," writes Norman Macfarlane, "was homely and quaint, with an extraordinary amount of sunshine and balmy air, while Mr Macrae carried the hurricane and the startling peal." And both were needed.

The great revival of 1859-60 which had brought such rich blessing to America had later symbolised its arrival in Ireland by numerous conversions there.

Tidings of events were arousing interest and deepening longing in many hearts in Scotland—John Macrae's among them. Preaching from the words in Psalm 68: 18, *"Thou hast ascended on high, Thou hast led captivity captive; Thou hast received gifts for men; yea, for the rebellious also, that the Lord God might dwell among them",* Mr Macrae said, "Perhaps the Holy Ghost is crossing the Irish Channel at this moment. God grant we may feel His power."

That prayer was almost immediately answered. Lochs, as well as other parts of Lewis, was soon in the grip of a mighty spiritual awakening. The numbers attending the church became so great that the services had to be held in the open. The spirit of repentance swept through the people. Convicted sinners cast themselves upon the forgiving mercy of Christ and entered into the peace that comes through believing. Forty young men were admitted to the communicant membership of the congregation, and still the tide of blessing flowed. Quite clearly, the providential circumstances that had sent John Macrae back to Lewis involved more than the health of the minister, God had a blessing prepared for the people of Lochs and His purpose was to send it by the hand of "MacRath Mor."

Of course there were critics of the movement, and in every spiritual awakening there is always something upon which the critics can fasten. Were there not some in Jerusalem who would have dismissed Pentecost itself with the sneer, "These men are full of new wine"? At a communion fellowship-meeting in Easter Ross one of the speakers seized the opportunity to pronounce unfavourable judgment upon the Lochs revival, and he had his supporters. But Angus Maciver, a convert of the Rev. Alexander Macleod in the earlier Uig awakening, happened to be present and, when recognised, was called upon to take part in the speaking. The criticisms of the Ross-shire brethren were given an immediate refutation by a man speaking from first-hand knowledge of the facts. Mr Macrae heard about the incident and dubbed the fault-finders "the black crows of Easter Ross!"

The species, alas, is not yet extinct, nor is it confined to one locality!

Among the crop of converts in Lochs at this time were some who became notable in the religious history of Lewis. Norman C. Macfarlane has given us thumb-nail sketches of some of them in his *The "Men" of Lewis*. The after-glow of the revival continued in the lives of these men, and the palates of the saints were often refreshed by their testimony.

Amidst the holy rejoicing of a time of revival, John Macrae's home was darkened by a desolating bereavement when his like-minded wife died. They had come together in romantic circumstances twenty-six years previously. She was then Penelope Mackenzie, the charming and godly daughter of Captain Thomas Mackenzie, tacksman at Bayble in Lewis. A friend of John's who had sought the hand and heart of Penelope, but without success, had hit upon the novel plan of sending John to plead his cause. The commission was eventually accepted and loyally acted upon but with no better success. Penelope had other thoughts, and suspected something that the pleader had not disclosed.

"Mr Macrae," she said at the parting, "all your appeals are for your friend. Have you no word to say for yourself?"

So charmingly prompted, and with the knowledge that there was no prospect of success for his friend, Mr Macrae *did* say a word for himself, and with better results. The romance blossomed into a marriage in which the parties were of one mind in the Lord. In the years of toil and hardship Mrs Macrae had been a tower of strength to her husband, and her death left him desolate. But her last testimony to the world softened and sanctified his mourning, for she died with the words of Isaiah upon her lips, *"I will greatly rejoice in the Lord, my soul shall be joyful in my God; for He hath clothed me with the garments of salvation, He hath covered me with the robe of righteousness, as a bridegroom decketh himself with ornaments, and as a bride adorneth herself with her jewels"* (Is. 61: 10).

The manner of her passing was itself a treasury of golden memory to her stricken husband, and it stimulated him to more abundant labours in the ministry of the Divine grace that could produce such consecrated character. But Lochs, with its widely scattered townships, its roadless moorlands and its multitudes of parishioners wore him down, and in 1866 he accepted a call to the less demanding congregation of Carloway.

Mr Macrae was now seventy years of age; but the people of the west side of Lewis desired the ripe fruits of his ministry—a desire which matched his own longing to serve to the utmost of his strength, and for so long as possible, the Master to Whom he owed so much.

Carloway had formed part of the congregation of Lochs before the Disruption, and for a short time thereafter. But in 1844 a new charge of Carloway and Callernish was sanctioned. Two years later, by the devoted exertions of a willing people, a church building was erected, but it was not until 1858 that the new charge had a minister of its own—the pastoral care of the people, in the interim, being entrusted to a catechist. The Rev. John Maclean, a native of Islay, became their first minister by his translation from Muckairn, and he remained with them until, in 1863, he accepted a call to Stratherrick.

John Macrae came next in the Carloway succession. The revival that had brought such rich blessing to Lochs seven years earlier had swept over this district also, and the parish was as "a field which the Lord had blessed." With, as it seemed, a fresh accession of strength, Mr Macrae threw himself into the work. But the bursts of brilliance that marked his Carloway ministry proved to be the last fitful gutterings of the almost-spent candle, and in 1871 he had to demit his charge. When he removed from Carloway to Stornoway he preached frequently in the old Free Church there, for it was vacant at the time. It became a memorable year for Stornoway, and a year of comfort for the ageing pastor himself as the Lord added to the church, in the closing phase of his Island ministry such as were being saved.

It was as the Psalmist had said:—

Those that within the house of God
*   are planted by His grace,*
They shall grow up, and flourish all
*   in our God's holy place.*

And in old age, when others fade,
*   they fruit still forth shall bring;*
They shall be fat, and full of sap,
*   and aye be flourishing.*

Chapter Six

THE SON OF CONSOLATION

The criticism is sometimes heard that old-time Scottish Presbyterianism gave little place to special evangelistic services and missions. Up to a point, the statement is true, and yet it can be very misleading. The fact is that Presbyterianism in Scotland was so structured as to ensure that evangelism was given its due place in the Church's normal activities. Evangelistic services and missions there were in abundance, but they were not described as "special." They took their planned place in the Church's life, principally by means of the communion seasons. Designedly, the observance of the Lord's Supper in the local congregation was an infrequent event. Sometimes the sacrament was dispensed only once in the year; seldom was it observed more than twice. One reason for this was the fear that too frequent communicating might result in an undue familiarity, resulting in a lessening of reverence for the ordinance. Considerations of domestic economy had their own influence, for it was customary for visitors from neighbouring parishes to gather at the various communions, and while hospitality was as lavish as circumstances permitted, those circumstances were sometimes straitened.

These great communion gatherings had the effect of extending the worshippers' interests beyond the bounds of their own particular parishes, and helped to develop a community spirit among congregations which, without these gatherings, would have had no meeting point.

The services of the communion season were spread over five days, from the Thursday of one week to the Monday of the next. Thursday was known as the Fast Day, although the ascetic element in its character had long disappeared. Its special theme was "Humiliation and Confession of Sin." Friday's theme was "Self-examination," and the principal gathering of the day was the "Question," or "Fellowship," meeting. One minister, almost invariably the senior, presided at the opening part of the meeting, and gave a brief exegesis of the particular passage of Scripture chosen for the day, and "given out" by one of the office-bearers present. Thereafter, office-bearers and male communicants, in the main from other congregations, were called upon to speak, and the "marks" of the true believer, which distinguished him from the religious pretender, were discussed. Another minister then "closed the question" by summing up what had been said, and correcting anything that might have been said amiss. The Friday evening service was expected to continue in the strain of experimental religion.

Saturday was the "Day of Preparation" for the sacrament, and the preaching of the day was related to that purpose.

The climax of the "season" was the Sabbath service at which the sacrament of the Supper was dispensed. The "action" sermon dealt with some aspect of Gospel reconciliation and atonement, and it was followed by the "fencing" of the

Lord's table, the object of which was to instruct the people as to the true nature of the holy ordinance, and to help the intending communicants with the duty of self-examination which is required of all who make public profession of the name of Christ. After the prayer of consecration, the presiding minister gave a special word of exhortation to the communicants before distributing the elements, and either he or another minister gave a closing word before the communicants left the tables. The evening service was evangelistic in character, and constituted a call to the unconverted.

The Thanksgiving Service followed on the Monday, and thereafter the congregation went their several ways, many in the frame of mind expressed by one of the godly women of Sutherland who used to say, at the parting, "Blessed be the Lord that there is no 'Monday' to the communion in heaven."

With such gatherings as these, so widely representative and so carefully planned, the criticism of old-time Scottish Presbyterianism — that it laid but little stress on evangelism and mission—surely falls to the ground.

The more popular ministers were in frequent demand for these communion services, and few, in his time, could have been more sought after than John Macrae. Where he was listed to appear there were sure to be great attendances. Mr Macmaster helps to give us the atmosphere of these gatherings. Mr Macrae's appearance, he tells us, "as he presented himself before a congregation at once arrested attention; it suggested to the hearers the thought that this was a messenger from God. Many in almost all parts of the world will remember services conducted by him, especially on Communion Sabbaths, when he appeared with his countenance radiant as one who had come down from the Mount of Communion, and how, by the time he had read the Psalm and engaged in prayer, the congregation, often consisting of many thousands, was awed into eager attention, and throughout an expression of delight appeared on the faces of God's people, while the most careless were solemnised, often deeply moved."

The fragments which have come down to us from his communion table addresses, in particular, reveal the tenderness of his heart towards the timid who feared that he might be unworthy of taking a place at the Master's table.

The custom of "fencing" the Lord's table has, nowadays, fallen into disfavour in the larger Presbyterian denominations in Scotland — an inevitable consequence of virtually indiscriminate admission to the sacrament of the Lord's Supper. It was not so in John Macrae's time. The apostolic injunction was faithfully urged, "Let a man examine himself and so let him eat of this bread and drink of this cup." Indeed, the opening words were inscribed on the communion token which the communicant brought with him to the sacramental table. The *Shorter Catechism* which, next to the Bible itself, was the principal manual of instruction in Presbyterian congregations, set forth in a helpful manner the plan of the self-examination desiderated. Intending communicants were to examine themselves as to "their knowledge to discern the Lord's body, their faith to feed upon Him, their repentance, love and new obedience, lest coming unworthily they eat and drink judgment to themselves, not discerning the Lord's body." It was recognised that "unworthy" communicating not only brought no blessing to the participant, but that it exposed him to positive harm and was dishonouring to the Lord. The fencing of the table was, therefore, designed to help the communicant in the exercise of self-scrutiny. For "the sacrament without the Spirit" — as Rutherford put it — "is no better than a piece of naked wax without seals." Now, it has to be admitted that there were occasions when the "fencing" largely failed of its purpose. The duty was sometimes performed harshly and even censoriously, with an excess of detail which was the reverse of helpful. Many good people, misapprehending what was really meant by "worthy" communicating, stayed away from the Lord's table altogether, fearing lest they should bring reproach upon the holy ordinance and judgment upon themselves.

The sketches of communion sermons and table addresses of John Macrae which have come down to us reveal his dread of setting a stumbling-block in the way of the timid believer, and his earnest desire to bring him into surrender and obedience to Him Who said: "This do in remembrance of Me." He was like-minded with James Macdonald, the catechist of Reay, of whom his son, Dr John Macdonald, wrote:

> *Never did he care to winnow*
> *with a wind that drove along,*
> *Lest its sudden gusts should sweep the*
> *precious wheat the chaff among;*

> *Rather far he thought it safe that*
> *chaff be left among the grain*
> *Than the smallest corn of wheat should*
> *with the worthless chaff remain.*

Take this extract, for example, from a communion address that he gave in Stornoway: "Friend, why are you so slow in coming forward to the table? Is it your reward you are hoping for? It is for you first to come and do your duty, and then you may claim, or plead, for your reward."

When the communicants had assembled at the Lord's table, he said: "There is no one here by right but one who has faith. I think I hear someone saying, 'If that is true, I have no title to be here, for my faith has gone away from me.' If so, I will tell you one thing you have, my friend: you have hope, and I compare you to a blind man going from door to door asking alms, with a boy leading him, as I used to see in the city when I was a young man. In like manner, your hope is leading you from door to door, from ordinance to ordinance, asking alms at Christ's door; and rest assured He will give you all He sees you need."

At another time, in inviting communicants to come to the Lord's table, he said: "Friend, come forward, though you should come on all fours. And I know, trembling soul, if there were a way underground by which you could come, you would take it so that you should not be seen approaching the holy table. Come, I again say to you, though you should do so creeping like a snail; but you must not, like the snail, leave a slimy trail behind you, or have immorality or carelessness polluting your daily life. And though you cannot come running in the way of God's commandments, as you would desire, still strive to come walking according to His Word as you are able, trusting to the grace and Spirit of God. For He has left us a parting and loving injunction which it is our duty to follow — 'This do in remembrance of Me.' "

Norman C. Macfarlane recalls hearing him at a communion service in Back. "I never heard tenderer words than his in the 'fencing,'" he says. "Is there one soul here," he said, "who cannot see the mark of Christ on himself. One who is like a sheep with a broken leg, unable to follow God's flock? Alas! you feel you cannot follow, but your wistful glance is after the flock. Come forward, poor trembler, and sit at your Lord's table. That wistful look is an inerrant token of your belonging to Christ."

On another occasion he was assisting his friend, the Rev Roderick Macleod, of Snizort, at a communion there, when the communicants still held back after having been twice invited by Mr Macleod to come forward. Mr Macrae stood up in the pulpit and said: "I am sorry, my friends, that, after being twice urged by my brother, you are still holding back from the table. It may be that you feel yourselves today as at an assize, with three witnesses accusing and condemning you in order to keep you from coming to the Lord's table. First, there is Satan, the accuser of the brethren, urging your unworthiness, for the purpose of working on your fears, and thus preventing your approach. The second witness is the world, urging this and that against you, and saying that you ought not come, and that it

49

would be presumptuous on your part to do so. The third witness is your own conscience, which sternly condemns you in many things wherein you are blameworthy and wrong. These three witnesses have combined to accuse you and deter you from coming to the Lord's table. But let me tell you, weary soul, that you have a Friend at court Who is more influential than all these, and Who is pleading for you against all your accusers. *And if any man sin, we have an advocate with the Father, Jesus Christ the righteous. Him the Father heareth always; the Spirit also Himself helpeth our infirmities, and maketh intercession for us with groanings which cannot be uttered.* Let me tell you, troubled one, that there are three on your side — the Father, the Son, and the Holy Spirit — and let me add that I myself would be pleased to see you approach, assured that your coming will be profitable to you; though there were no more than this urging you and pressing on your spirit, 'This do in remembrance of Me.' Ye who have truly centred your hope in the grace of God, be of good courage, and He will impart life and strength unto your souls."

Comforted and encouraged by these words, the communicants delayed no longer and the Lord's table was "furnished with guests." Nicol Nicolson writes that an elder who was present on that occasion in Snizort told him that he had never seen communicants so powerfully influenced as they were by Mr Macrae's pleadings on that occasion. "He and others arose as if a warm and strengthening gale, or a breath like the blessed breath of the Spirit of God had passed over the congregation." Mr Nicolson refers also

to a communion table address that he himself
had heard from Mr Macrae at Barvas in 1861.
"He spoke thus," writes Mr Nicolson,
"Communicant, I am going to mention four
things at this time, and, if you have them, I take
it upon myself to say that they will bring you to
Glory. The first I shall mention is, that you were
enabled at one time or another to say in any
measure, as the Church says in the Song, 'My
Beloved is mine, and I am His.' Christ, you
believed, had given Himself to you as the object
of your soul's desire, and you felt as if you had
been led to consecrate yourself, body and soul, to
Him, and to live for Him alone, as if you had
said, *I am my Beloved's, and my Beloved is
mine.*' Christ is mine, and I am Christ's; I
received Christ when He received me; He is all in
all to me.' If you were enabled in any measure to
say this, the next thing which follows from it, and
which I shall name, is, that you felt the love of
Christ filling you with a strong and fixed desire to
say, or do, something for Christ in any possible
form; like the woman of Samaria, whom Christ
met at the well, who went home, leaving her
water-pot behind her, and said to the people of
the city, 'Come, see a man which told me all
things that ever I did,' adding, 'Is not this the
Christ?' The first two things, I admit, are
undoubtedly great, but the third thing which I
am about to mention is, I am satisfied, easier for
you, burdened soul, to adopt. It is what the
Psalmist says: 'As the hart panteth after the water-
brooks, so panteth my soul after Thee, O God; my
soul thirsteth for God, the living God.'

"Your soul today needs as much as ever it

51

did, or more than you were ever conscious of its needing, to know God as your own living God, for Whom your thirsting soul is constantly panting.

"The fourth thing I shall mention is this: when you, believing one, have duties to perform, difficulties to encounter, wants to satisfy, temptations to overcome, sins to crucify, you anxiously ask: 'How can I be sufficient for all this, and what provision has been made for these things?' The self-same provision which was promised to Paul, and which completely met his case, when he besought the Lord that he would relieve him of his trouble — 'My grace is sufficient for thee, for My strength is made perfect in thy weakness.' This grace is sufficient to enable you to fulfil every duty. This grace is sufficient to carry you through every difficulty. This grace is sufficient to supply all your need. This grace is sufficient to enable you to overcome all the temptations of the evil one. This grace is sufficient to mortify and consume all the indwelling sin that burdens your soul, and to lead you safely at last into the haven of glory."

At the close of a communion service he quoted our Lord's words: "Arise, let us go hence," and used them as an expression of Christ's devotion to the duty entrusted to Him by the Father. "Christ," he said, "had more regard to the Father's command than to the society of the disciples, pleasant though that was."

But there was a special word for those who might be arising and departing without conscious benefit. "Afflicted one, you are perhaps lamenting, 'I am returning home from the

ordinance without receiving any spiritual benefit.'
If you have made the acquaintance of one of
God's people whom you had not known before,
let me assure you that that is a token that you
have received spiritual good. And if there is a
stronger desire in your soul to go to the next
communion, that also proves that your soul has
been benefited."

Speaking from the words in Isaiah 48: 18: *"O
that thou hadst hearkened to my commandments!
then had thy peace been as a river, and thy
righteousness as the waves of the sea,"* he
commented: "Thy peace would be like a river,
flowing gracefully, abundantly, proudly, and for
ever. That is the disposition promised in these
words. And, again, thy righteousness would be as
the waves of the sea, like the waves which you
can see in the dim distance coming across from
Gairloch Point, one after another, rolling
smoothly, steadily, irresistibly, incessantly and
unweariedly, till they break on the rocks at Cabag
Head. Nothing can obstruct, or break, or turn
the waves till they have run their course. So it is
with the righteousness of the gracious soul;
nothing that the soul may encounter in the world
will change, or obstruct, or break it — once
justified, His righteousness endureth for ever."

The "meek and quiet voice" that sounded in the
prophetic ear of Lachlan Mackenzie when he
foretold the conversion and ministry of John
Macrae came to articulation in these tender
passages from his preaching. His words were as
"rain upon the mown grass" in the experience of
many of his hearers. They looked to God, and the
glory of His grace broke upon them.

53

Great God of wonders! All Thy ways
Are worthy of Thyself—Divine;
But the bright glories of Thy grace
Beyond all other wonders shine.
Who is a pardoning God like Thee,
Or who has grace so rich and free?

Chapter Seven

A BASKET OF FRAGMENTS

Mr Macrae belonged to an age when the reading of sermons from the pulpit was not in favour. The practice was more common in the Established Church than in the Free Church, or the other dissenting bodies. There were notable exceptions, of course, prominent among them Dr Thomas Chalmers and Dr Hugh Martin, whose sermons lost nothing in eloquence and popular appeal from the fact that they were preached from manuscript. But, generally speaking, "paper preaching" was at a decided discount in the Free Church; they left that to the Moderates! Nicol Nicolson tells of a visit that "Big Macrae" paid to Tiree during the post-Disruption period when, on a Monday evening, he addressed the people on the questions that were agitating the Church at the time. The local Established Church minister appeared at the close of the meeting with a written paper in his hand which he proceeded to read, when Mr Macrae broke in, "See that poor man going to read what probably he was busy writing yesterday!"

This sly dig at the ways of the Moderates raised a laugh against the defender of the Establishment, and, realising that he had lost the day, he retreated in discomfiture. The result of the meeting may be judged from the fact that the hill on which it took place was known thereafter as "Cnoc Mhic-rath" (Macrae's Hill) in honour of the visitor. Like Caesar, he came, he saw, he conquered!

The unfortunate result of the disdain of sermon manuscript, however, was that much of the best preaching of the time was lost to posterity. Some of the ministers did indeed write out their sermons, and although the manuscripts were never admitted to the pulpit, they were filed away in the manse study and later became available for publication. The harvest of Mr Macrae's literary labours, however, is light, and only the gleanings of his preaching remain. The two-volume study Bible that he used, principally in his Carloway ministry, has, by the kindness of two of his descendants, been in my possession for prolonged periods, and it has often proved a rewarding experience to try and follow the trend of his thought by pondering the notes which appear in his script on the inter-leaves of this Bible. It goes without saying that they do little to account for the extraordinary power and popularity of his preaching. They give us the merest hints of what he was thinking, and were obviously never meant to see the light of day. But we have included a few of these outlines in this book as means whereby we may form some impression of his exegetical and homiletical ability.

What these outlines do show with the utmost clarity is that his theology was of the authentic Reformed strain. Christ is set forth as the Son of God and the Saviour of His people. His Cross marks the mercy-seat where a gracious God, Who has no pleasure in the death of the wicked, dispenses mercy and grace to all who plead the merits of His propitiation.

His blood is the only, but ever-potent, cleanser from all sin. From first to last the emphasis is upon saving grace. The only permissible ground of boasting is the Cross; the only warrant of assurance of salvation is sovereign electing grace. There is no shunning to declare the whole counsel of God. The righteous is assured that it shall be well with him, but with equal plainness the wicked is warned that it shall be ill with him unless he humbles himself in penitence and accepts the amnesty of Calvary.

But these sermon outlines are, at the best, mere skeletons which he clothed with flesh and sinews as he went along. In his latter years his preaching mellowed considerably. To a young minister he once confessed, "When I was younger I used to think it was the thunder that struck things to earth; but now I see it is the lightning. I wish to thunder less and lighten more."

Often, his words had a burning intensity that left an indelible imprint upon the minds of his hearers and to this fact must, in part at least, be attributed the wealth of "MacRath Mor" memorabilia that is still available in the parts of the country that knew him best.

Some of these have already been recorded in these pages. The following are worthy of being added.

Speaking on one occasion, of the satisfaction rendered to the Divine attributes in the death of Christ, he put it like this: "No attribute of God was stronger than love, for love overcame God Himself. The law demanded perfect obedience from Christ. The law sent Him thrice to His knees in the garden of Gethsemane. Christ may be supposed to have said 'Will that suffice?' the law answering, 'No; this alone will satisfy me—my curse upon Thee, my curse upon Thee; death to Thee, death to Thee.'"

On another occasion, preaching from the words, *"For, verily, He took not on Him the nature of angels; but He took on Him the seed of Abraham* (Hebrews 2: 16)," he said, "Christ's taking of our nature recalls to my mind a story which used to be told in my native district. It was related that there was an old woman at Loch Duich side who used to kindle fires on the sheltered side of the loch, and when the wind shifted and blew against the fire she would take it up in her palm and hand it across to the other side of the loch, about the distance of a mile! What a reach! But, to speak with reverence, what a reach Christ had when He, Who had His home in heaven, came down and took over nature on earth! Or, to take another illustration; suppose you saw a lofty, precipitous steep above the sea, and that a large stone broke loose from its summit and came tumbling down, each fresh leap adding to its velocity and force, until, at last, it bounded into the depth of the sea. Now, what Christ did was this—He took our nature, which was like that stone, hurling down the steep of the fall to the depths of misery, bottomless and unending, but for the almighty arm of Christ which was stretched out to rescue and save from eternal destruction."

Referring to the relations of Faith and Hope in the soul of the believer, he put it like this. "I compare Faith to the head of the house, who bears all the burden and care of the family; and who is constantly seeking to provide for them; and Hope to a thrifty housewife who makes good use of her husband's earnings. Many a time Faith can bring nothing home for his family, and they might perish with want were it not that Hope, like a wise and prudent housewife, lays something aside to provide for the household when the husband is unable to earn anything."

But Hope herself had her times of feebleness and incapacity, and Faith then had to minister to Hope.

"The graces of the Spirit in the soul of the believer," he said, "are sometimes like a family smitten with a sore fever. Hope herself is down with the disease, and keeps up the cry, 'O give me a drink, or I shall die.' Faith comes to the window and listens. And having heard Hope's cry, he says, 'I must go and find a drink for Hope.'

"Back he comes with this drink for his stricken companion, *'The Lord your God . . . is gracious and merciful, slow to anger, and of great kindness, and repenteth Him of the evil. Who knoweth if He will return and repent, and leave a blessing behind Him?' "* (Joel 2: 13-14).

"Hope gets up to her elbow. 'I'm the better for that,' she says. But soon she is prostrate again; and, in high fever, cries, 'Fetch me a drink or I shall die.'

"Faith again looked in at the window, and saw how poorly Hope was. He comes with another drink, which he raises to Hope's lips. 'Take this,' he counsels; *'The Lord is my portion, saith my soul; therefore will I hope in Him.'* (Lam. 3: 24).

"Hope now springs to her feet with restored strength. 'I'm the better for that,' she cries; and she is soon busy in the affairs of the household, and joy and good cheer are soon restored to all the sick graces of the soul."

The following comment on the all-surpassing preciousness of Christ is worth recording. Speaking on the words of Andrew, "We have found the Messiah," and of the lasting blessedness of all who can join in that testimony, he said, "How destitute I see you — you who have not Christ. And you would still be destitute even if you possessed three things which you can never have together: I. All the worldly prosperity that you could ever desire; II. Your family all grown up around you, and doing well for themselves; and III. You yourself still in the full vigour and exuberance of youth. Death and hell-fire would soon deprive you of all such possessions, but the man who can truly say, 'I have found the Messiah,' has come into possession of the richest of all portions — a portion that shall be his for ever."

At the fellowship meetings it was customary, in discussing Christian experience to ask for the "marks" which distinguished the sincere believer from the religious sham. This was how "Big Macrae" once put it, "I resemble the true believer, in the dawn of his Christian experience, to the fledgling of the lark. Yonder it is in the nest, unable to do anything for itself but to open its beak for the food that its mother brings it. And I resemble the hypocrite in his beginnings to the chick of the hen. As soon as it is out of the shell it is on to the floor scratching away for itself. But let a year pass. Where is the young of the lark now? High up and out of sight, singing most sweetly. But where is the hen's chick now? Just where it was a year ago, scratching away on the dunghill."

Homely figures, but helpful illustrations for a simple people.

"My fellow-sinners," he urged on another occasion, "do not abuse the mercy of God; do not treat it as a common thing by imagining, or saying, 'Oh, the mercy of God is great, and He will not suffer us to be lost for ever.' Oh, do not abuse the mercy of God; do not presume upon God's mercy toward you in this world. I compare God's mercy, if I may so speak, to a gentlewoman. When our Queen used to visit our country a scarlet carpet was laid for her feet, between the stopping-place of the carriage that brought her from England and the door of the house where she was to stay, so that she might not set her foot on the ground or touch the common earth. In like manner, God's mercy is so fastidious that she will not set her foot on any place less worthy than the scarlet carpet of the merits of Christ's blood; and the sinner that will not meet with her on that ground, let him not expect that she will ever meet with him on the general course or pathway of his own sinful life in this world."

Ministering, as he did, at a time when a "Moderate" ministry failed to resist the encroachments of the State upon the government of the Kingdom of Christ, it was inevitable that his sermons should, on occasions, reflect the contemporary situation. Dealing, once, with the disloyalty of the Church to Christ her King, he spoke of the Lord as bringing a complaint to the Father regarding her lack of love and sense of duty to Him, and her shameful departure from Him. The Father's reply was, "Wait Thou, My Son, till we cast her into the stormy sea of tribulation. Before she sinks to the black rocks in the depths her heart will return to Thee."

Thus are the desertions of Christ's Bride corrected. And to her tears of penitence He is not indifferent.

Commenting on the words, *"They shall look on Him whom they pierced."* (John 19: 37) he said, "Every sin is a shaft. Every one pierces Christ. But there is one sin that has a double barb — the sin of unbelief. With this shaft sinners endeavour to pierce Christ under the fifth rib."

In urging his people to give liberally to missions among the Jews, who, in a special manner, pierced Christ by their unbelieving rejection of Him, he stressed the willingness of Christ to forgive and restore, and said, "I earnestly beseech you to give liberally to this good object, as the Lord will be pleased with you for doing so. If you had a disobedient son who would not stay with you, but ran away from home, you would esteem anyone who showed kindness to him, though he was disobedient to you. Though the Jews are enemies concerning the Gospel, yet they are beloved for their fathers' sake."

Preaching in his native Kintail, on one occasion, he referred to the all-too-prevalent folly of providing for everything except the soul. "I remember," he said, "when food was scarce in

Kintail, the man of the house would go out in the morning to see what he could find for the family. If he was successful in his hunting, the housewife would prepare a meal for the family. There would be a portion for her husband, a portion for each child, and a portion for herself. But there would be no portion for the dog. Not only so, but the dog would be put outside lest it should seize upon the portion of any of the family. It would have to prowl for itself, and find what it could.

"My friend, be very careful not to treat your soul in that way."

Referring to the spirit of surrender and consecration that ought to characterise every believer, he put it like this. "Suppose the Queen should so humble herself as to visit a poor woman, who lived in a sooty house, and spend a time of fellowship with her. At the Queen's departure the poor woman might say, 'I have nothing to give the Queen that is worthy of her acceptance, but this I will do; the stool on which you sat, O Queen, no other shall ever use it. It will be kept here for your use if at any time you should be pleased to come again.'"

Speaking of the temptations that trouble the believer, he remarked, "Methinks I saw the world of men as sheep asleep in the valley while Satan came against them with the hounds of hell. But it was to a small flock on the hillside that Satan gave his first attention. 'Don't disturb the sheep that are asleep,' he charged his hounds. 'Yonder is the flock that give me concern. Go and catch *them*, and, if you cannot kill them, at least tear them and make their lives bitter.'

"The dogs made for them, but the Lord was

as a wall of fire around them, and as a glory in the midst of them. The hounds returned to their master, and he turned away almost choked with rage over his failure."

These fragments from his preaching show that Mr Macrae found his illustrations, for the most part, in everyday life and commonplace happenings. Speaking on the Monday of a communion season in the Isle of Skye, of the reward of the Christian servant at his home-coming, he said, "There is a custom in our islands that when a housewife wishes to hatch a brood of chickens, if she does not have a broody hen of her own at the time she will look around and borrow one from a neighbour who may happen to have one that she is not then needing. And when the chicks are produced the grateful housewife will duly return the borrowed hen to her owner, with a chicken under each wing in gratitude. But, oh, what a joyful homecoming it would be for me if I came with even one chick under my wing!"

There was a touch of Samuel Rutherford there.

> Oh! if one soul from Anwoth
>   Meet me at God's right hand
> My Heaven will be two Heavens
>   In Immanuel's Land.

Preaching once in Shieldaig on the words "... *in whom we have redemption through His blood* ..." (Ephes. 1: 7), he posed the question, "Who are these redeemed ones?" The law had pursued and arrested them as transgressors, and they were cast into the prison of Justice. "Do you remember, my friend, the clang of the prison gate when Justice closed it? You were closed in to gaze through the prison bars at the awful eternity that awaited you, without any prospect of change. But Christ came that day to visit Justice. 'What is Thy business with me today?' asked Justice.

"'I am come,' said Christ, 'to see if you will give me the key of the prison, so that I may release those poor creatures.'

"But Justice shook his head against Christ's proposal, and, for a little, was quite speechless. When speech returned, he said, 'What will you give me for the key?'

"'I will give you,' said Christ, 'a ransom of blood, for I know that, according to our rules, the key cannot be exchanged for anything else.'

"The key was then given, and how long, think you, did it take Christ to pay that ransom of blood? It took thirty-three years, and He left footprints of blood behind Him at every step of the way."

Commenting on the words *"A friend loveth at all times,"* (Provs. 17: 17), he said, "Great was the bondage of the human race in the prison of law and justice. No wonder if hearts should be melted with love to the brother who set the sinner free from it."

Speaking of the desolation caused by the Flood, and the sending out of the raven by Noah when the waters were abating, he said, "That bird never cared so much for the world as he did then, for he had a large number of dead carcases to feed upon. So it is with the wicked. They are never so happy as when there is spiritual death in the world, and when no one reproves them for

65

E

their wickedness. Beware, ye wicked, when a saint is taken home, if the Lord does not raise up another in his place. But the dove found no rest and never left the Ark, but remained flying round about it. When once the soul has become united to Christ many a time it would, if it were possible, snatch itself away from everything to be with Him, and with Him alone."

In a sermon on the words, *"The Father loveth the Son, and hath given all things into His hand,"* (John 3: 35), he represented the Father as discussing with the Son the mission on which He proposed sending Him into the world, and as showing Him the people amongst whom He was to come. "Look," said the Father, "those are the people. Lost they are, and lost they must ever remain unless Thou dost undertake for them. Wilt Thou go to their help?"

The Son replied, "I delight to do Thy will, O My God."

"But if Thou wilt go," said the Father, "Thou must partake of their nature. Wilt Thou now go My Son?"

He replied, "I delight to do Thy will, O My God,"

"But if you go in their nature, they will spit upon Thee. Wilt Thou now go, My Son?"

Again He replied, "I delight to do Thy will, O My God."

"But if Thou wilt go, they will put Thee to death. Wilt Thou still go, My Son?"

Again He replied, "I delight to do Thy will, O My God."

When the Father heard this, He produced the great keys of authority, and gave them to the

Son, saying, "Take then the keys, and My blessing with them. For the Father loveth the Son, and hath given all things into His hand."

"According to the Scriptures," he remarked on another occasion, "the broken heart comes from a sight of Christ crucified for sin. The soul, by faith beholding the cross, sees God's hatred to sin and yet His love for the sinner, in that He spared not the Son of His love when no other means would serve His purpose of redemption. He gave the Son of His love to be bruised and broken for sin, even to death, in the place of sinners who deserved eternal sufferings for their . offences. He was bruised and broken between the upper and nether mill-stones, or, in other words, between the inflexible Justice of God and the holy, unchangeable, everlasting Love of God. God's holy, unchanging Love bore Him up against the strokes, and His Justice kept bruising and breaking Him to death until Justice was fully satisfied. Then Jesus cried, 'It is finished,' and He gave up the ghost. I venture to say that that was the hour when sin came nearest to the essence of Deity."

Christ's presence in heaven as the believer's representative with the Father was a favourite theme. Therein lies the Christian's hope for eternity. "Some good men," he said, "think Christ is coming to reign on a throne in the earthly Jerusalem. It is better for me that He should continue to reign where He is."

Yet he knew in personal experience the longing of the believer for the coming again of Christ. Quoting the words in Luke 24: 50, *"He led them out as far as to Bethany,"* he commented: "The eyes of the disciples were toward Him as He ascended, and, ever since, the eyes of all His people gaze heavenwards after Him."

By various figures and metaphors he stressed the complete reliability of Christ's Saviourhood. "When fishermen launch a boat, and it is afloat," he once remarked, "they say, 'It is now on the great burden-bearer.' Let it be so with your soul. Launch it upon Christ, and He will be the great burden-bearer for you."

In a sermon preached from the words of Isaiah 45: 22, *"Look unto Me and be ye saved, all the ends of the earth . . ."* Mr Macrae cried, "O in God's Name look to Him and be saved. You sit before me still unsaved, some of you for twenty years, yes, and some for eighty years, on your way to eternal destruction as swiftly as the wings of Time can bear you. O will you not look to the Eternal Godhead in the depth of the manger! O will you not bend over Him and look until He brings down your haughty look and your proud spirit! What is He doing, lying there? He is working out salvation for your soul. O, will you not look to Him again covered with spittles; His hair plucked out by the hands of His enemies! O, will you not look to Him in His sweat of blood! O, devils, begone to hell, there is no offer here for you. O, my fellow-sinners, it is not to you that I refer, but to the devilish spirits that dance upon your spirit before me. I do not disparage the lamentations of my fellow-sinners; far be it from me. But let me say this to you. Should your eyes drop from their sockets through sorrow, and

68

should your knees become horny through praying, that will not save you.

"Who then can be saved? I can tell you that. It is everyone who confesses and forsakes his sin, everyone who perseveres to the end, — these shall be saved. 'But, O,' says the aged man, 'there is no salvation for me; I have given all the days of my life to the service of the devil, the enemy of my soul; my heart has become stony; my head is now withered, and I cannot now sorrow unto repentance. There is nothing for me but to be lost.'

"O, my fellow-sinner, do not say such things. There is a 'stove' yonder to prepare the wood that goes to the making of the great ships. The stubborn wood comes out subdued, and is ready to be prepared for its place in the hull of the ship. And when your soul, my friend, is plunged into the intense heat of a Saviour's love, it will become as pliable as a twig of willow. When the fire of prayer is kindled upon the hearth of your soul by the Holy Spirit, there is no secret place or hill-cleft of which you will not avail yourself to fall down before the presence of God. And neither time nor eternity will make an end of this new communion and submissiveness."

At a fellowship meeting over which he presided on one occasion, the passage given out for discussion was, *"I will also leave in the midst of thee an afflicted and poor people and they shall trust in the name of the Lord,"* (Zeph. 3: 12). Commenting on these words, he said: "As meat that has not been salted goes to waste, so it is with the world. It would putrify and go to waste were it not for the presence of God's people, which acts as its preserving salt. And the storms and troubles which they encounter drive them to Himself. Were it not for this they would wax cold and dead and indifferent about Him; and when the soul cries to God in time of trouble, He hears and says, 'Hasten home, My child.' "

Three of Mr Macrae's biographers had heard him preach, and they have given us interesting impressions of him as he appeared in the pulpit, and the general effect that his preaching produced. Donald Macmaster's impressions we have already quoted. Those of Norman C. Macfarlane come obviously from a much younger hearer. "In appearance he was big and tall," he writes. "In many a house the ceiling must have sat on his head. His head was large and he wore a dark brown wig. When he put up his hands and pulled the wig down closer to his ears we knew he was clearing the decks for a rush. Inspirations which he could not resist came upon him. He was in the grip of an angel who stirred the waters and then rose a tumultuous surge of splendour. He was thrilled himself under the onrush and he thrilled others and awed them. His forehead which was lofty had angles. His eyes had pouches underneath. His nose was Roman. The usual photograph of him is full-face, but a profile would be more striking. A fringe of whisker framed his face. His lower lip was somewhat heavily moulded. The upper lip was firm. He carried no spare flesh on his face. His size and walk arrested attention."

After his retirement from Carloway, Mr Macrae lived for a year in Stornoway, where he preached once every Sabbath in the old Free Church which was vacant at the time. "That year," writes Mr Macfarlane, "in point of preaching was the greatest that Stornoway ever had. Sabbath after Sabbath men were lifted into wonderlands, and left the service amazed at the undreamt glories of Christ and His Gospel. Mr Macrae's Communion services were always memorable, but one he preached in the old Free Church seminary on 'Christ's Banqueting House' was unsurpassable. The holy passion, the lofty thought, the poetry, the beauty, the flight of imagination, and the touches of exquisite tenderness made it the greatest public utterance I have ever heard. The preacher awed us. His rapt soul made him like Enoch, one who walked with God. His diction was extraordinarily graphic and terse. It seemed as if preaching had reached its highest heights that day. For years I carried about with me notes of the sermon, but no notes could possibly convey a tithe of the impression which was made by the overwhelming majesty of the preacher."

Nicol Nicolson's tribute to Mr Macrae as a preacher of the Gospel has to be evaluated in the light of his disclosure that he was as he put it, "more indebted to Mr Macrae than to all whom we have been privileged to hear of God's most honoured servants. We have listened more than once to Dr Mackintosh of Dunoon; Mr Roderick Macleod, of Snizort; Mr Spurgeon, and many other eminent men, but, in our opinion, he surpassed them all in point of substance. animation, power, fulness, and impressiveness."

This comparison of giants is probably biassed

by the fact that although a believer may have "ten thousand instructers in Christ," yet he has not "many fathers" (I Cor. 4: 15). But Mr Nicolson undoubtedly pinpoints one great advantage that John Macrae had as a preacher, and that was a vivid imagination. This, says Mr Nicolson, "was effectively employed by him in emblematical illustrations, and in the use of natural phenomena and apposite anecdotes, to elucidate and enforce spiritual truth. He could thus arrest the attention of people of various dispositions, they were able to carry with them more of his teaching than that of most men, and by the manner, as well as by the matter, of his appeals, he made a deep impression on the minds of his hearers. Whatever subject he handled, he rendered clear and intelligible to the meanest and least gifted in the congregation. This was one of his most conspicuous endowments, and it was a matter of wonder to many how easily the darkest and most abstruse points became clear under his masterly treatment."

To put it in modern parlance, John Macrae had, in a marked degree, the gift of communication. The use of illustration and allegory, of anecdote and aphorism, was not common among the preachers of his day. Some of them produced sermons which Principal John Macleod once described as "well-built and finely furnished houses that were nevertheless defective in that they had not been fitted with windows!"

On the evidence of his hearers, John Macrae was at pains to let in the light. Coming from a master pulpiteer, passages like the following would arrest the attention, illumine the mind, and drive home the lesson.

Speaking of the prevalency and subtlety of temptation, he remarked, "I compare the Christian, in his perilous journey through this world, to a man walking along a narrow passage between two rows of close fires, with a sack of gunpowder on his back. He must be careful at every step that he does not go nearer to one side or the other, that the smallest spark from the fire should touch the powder and blow him to pieces."

And as an additional incentive to a circumspect walk he once added the following. "If you ask what it was that caused Christ the sorest strokes from the sword of Divine justice, I would answer that it was the sins committed by His people after being made His by faith."

When he quoted Divine promises he was careful to remind his hearers that they were not common property. Preaching on the words, *"Thy sun shall no more go down, neither shall thy moon withdraw itself,"* (Isaiah 60: 20), he linked with that gracious assurance the words of the next verse, *"Thy people also shall be all righteous;"* and asked, "Why did the Lord set down this truth immediately after such a great promise? I venture to think it was in order that no hypocrite should lay hold, or presume to lay hold, on such a promise."

Sometimes Mr Macrae resorted to allegorical interpretations of Scripture, but only with such passages as are allegorical in character themselves. It is a method that has to be followed with the utmost care, lest the result should be a

73

travesty of the Word. Mr Macrae, however, was a master of the art of spiritualising, as may be gathered from the foregoing selections from his preaching. The outline of his sermon on Solomon's Chariot, which has been included in the sermon summaries which appear at the end of this biography, will give some impression of his skill in this line of preaching.

A common feature of all his preaching was his emphasis on the power of Divine grace. The testimony of the erstwhile persecutor who became an apostle would have suited his experience. "By the grace of God I am what what I am." Like the converted slave-trader, John Newton, he could have said:

> 'Twas grace that taught my heart to fear,
>   And grace my fears relieved;
> How precious did that grace appear
>   The hour I first believed.
> Through many dangers, toils and snares
>   I have already come;
> 'Tis grace has brought me safe thus far,
>   And grace will lead me home.

The power of grace, he said, was beyond all calculation. Even "a spark of grace," falling into the ocean of man's corruption, would retain all its power of survival. Indeed, not only would it not be extinguished by the floods of corruption around it, it would eventually dry up that ocean altogether.

But the security of the believer, which is such a cause of rejoicing in heaven is differently regarded in hell. Norman C. Macfarlane recalls a sermon preached by Mr Macrae in which he spoke of the final security of God's ransomed. "There were many passages of beauty," he recalls. "One was a grim picture of Satan. Mr Macrae seemed to walk the floors of Hell, when, suddenly, he espied Satan, whom he called the Hound of the Pit, addressing his angels; 'O devils, devils, God has triumphed, and we are crushed. Our arts and wiles, our sword-thrusts and poison-stings have all failed. Not one of the ransomed have we captured or slain. It comforts me little that we have many others. Mourn with me, O devils, over this dismal and eternal loss.'

"During this indescribable outburst one felt a quivering between the shoulder-blades and an icy stream down the spine, and all one's hair rising like quills. The scene in Hell was so vividly visualised that the very fumes of the Pit seemed to stifle us. Mr Macrae sprang from this Inferno to the glories of Heaven, and his face kindled with radiance. Our poor rigid limbs eased off into the most delicious relaxation, and a sigh of relief broke on the air. Across more than fifty years I still feel the awe and splendour of that hour."

It surely required a true master of assemblies to produce such an effect.

The flights of imagination that were such a feature of Mr Macrae's preaching reveal not only the depth of his spiritual understanding but also his gift of spiritual analysis. Here was a man who could speak home to the hearts of his hearers, a man of like passions, with themselves, a Greatheart who knew the heights and depths of Christian experience, and who was thereby specially qualified to guide them along the pilgrim way to the Celestial City.

Here we have him in one of his softer moods, speaking a word in season to the weary.

"Methinks I see an angel in the presence of the heavenly throne, listening to the plaintive prayer of a troubled saint on earth, and saying to the Almighty, 'Who is that whose plaint I hear?'

" 'That,' said the Lord, 'is one whose plaint is sweeter to Me than the music of the angels.'

" 'But wilt Thou not then give her a comforting drop out of the ocean of Thy love?'

" 'I will indeed do that,' said the Lord.

" 'And wilt Thou not give her more and more in such measure that she will be filled?'

" 'If I did that,' was the reply, 'she would cease from her plaintive prayers, and I would lose My music.' "

And the preacher went on to show how beneficial to the petitioner herself was this longing for holiness, and how fully the longing would be fulfilled when the trials of life are over, and the believer is finally brought home to the Father's house of many mansions.

Addressing the afflicted believers in his audience, on another occasion, he said "Your trials are like a strong wind blowing on a healthy tree, which is strengthened and not weakened, by the strain. Not only will the force of the adversity give exercise to all your graces, resulting in your greater fruitfulness, but it will also teach you to bow your head in Christian submission. In such storms the dead tree will break and fall, but not such as have in them the sap of grace."

The preacher knew from personal experience the benefit of sanctified affliction. A brother minister remarked to him one day as they were

76

passing through a pleasant and peaceful countryside in Lewis, "What a suitable place for prayer this would be." "Yes," replied Mr Macrae, *"but the deck of a battleship would be a better place by far."*

Prayer-life is never at its best in a hothouse. The temple of Janus at Rome, so it is said, was open in time of war, but shut in time of peace. Men were ready to flee to it when danger threatened, but when all was well the shrine was neglected; no offerings were brought to its altar. Unhappily, the same tendency is only too clearly discernible in lands where Christianity has long been the professed religion. We need the stress and strain of spiritual warfare and adverse providence to bring us to the throne of grace, and give to our supplications the qualities of importunity and earnest longing that the God, to Whom they are addressed, desires to see in them.

Chapter Eight

THE PASTOR AMONG HIS PEOPLE

It would be difficult to find material from which to present a portrait of Mr Macrae as a pastor among his people. Pastoral visitation was not so marked a part of a minister's work in those days as it has become in more recent times, and, in any case, to maintain close contact with the people — especially in the large congregations to which, for the most part, Mr Macrae ministered—was an utter impossibility. Means of communication and transport were difficult, and when many demands were made upon ministers by the Church authorities, as well as by brethren desiring communion assistance, there was even less time for the more intimate fellowship between pastor and people that is so essential to an effective ministry in more modern times. But what Mr Macrae lacked through these disadvantages was made less serious by his natural shrewdness, and his knowledge of human nature.

His commonsense in dealing with spiritual problems was frequently put to the test. One good man, Donald Morrison, who had recently been converted, sought his advice in a matter that was distressing him. He felt that his early morning devotions were not receiving proper attention on account of his pre-occupation with fishing. Ought he to give up his work in the interests of his spiritual advancement?

"Have you prayed, Donald," asked Mr Macrae, "for God's guidance in this matter?"

Donald could not claim that he had.

"Then," said his minister, "go home and do so, for it may well be the Lord's will that you should continue your fishing for the sake of your family and others."

Donald did as he had been directed, asking for a clear token from God as to what was his duty. He had been praying at the water's edge, and when he opened his eyes he saw a sea-buoy that had not been there when he had begun his prayer. This was God's token to him of where his duty lay. He was to continue his seafaring. That was the message of the buoy!

And Donald blessed his minister whose counsel had sent him to his knees for guidance.

Once, during his Greenock ministry a young man came to him to tell him of a spiritual problem that was troubling him. It was that he could not reconcile the free offer of the Gospel with predestination.

After a pause, Mr Macrae replied, "My young man, I resemble you to a sheep in a good pasture which, because it saw a clump of good grass on a rocky, perilous slope, left the safe pasture in order to get a mouthful of the grass that was growing in dangerous surroundings. Who are you, that you presume to enter upon mysteries which the Lord has been pleased to hide from human eyes?"

The young enquirer appreciated the wisdom of his minister's answer, and made it his rule thereafter to confine himself to the things which the Lord has revealed.

Mr Macrae had a tender spirit toward the sincere believer, but the sanctimonious sham fared ill at his hands. One of this sort came to him in simulated sorrow, weeping copious tears.

"What is the matter with you?" asked Macrae.

"I'm afraid," came the whimpering cry, "that the devil will have me some day."

"Some day!" echoed Mr Macrae, "You play-actor, the devil has you now."

On another occasion, crossing an arm of the sea to a week-day service, he became irritated by the ceaseless, empty chatter of a woman in the company. At one point, she turned the discussion to the Book of Revelation and, obviously desiring to impress the minister, asked him what was meant in chapter 8, v. 1 by the half-hour silence in heaven. The reply was unexpected. "My good woman, if you were there, there would be no silence!"

A Sustentation Fund collector once complained to him of the small contributions he received from some of the people. But John Macrae had his size. "Well," said he, "what do you give yourself?"

Evading the unexpected thrust, the denigrator of his brethren replied, "Oh, the Lord has not given me much of this world's wealth."

"The Lord was wise," came the devastating rejoinder.

Empty compliments he disdained. "Oh, Mr Macrae," said a young hearer, "that was a glorious sermon this morning. We must bring our souls up to this evening's service."

"Bring your ears, sir, bring your ears, don't forget them," was the reply.

An elder who patronisingly complimented him on a sermon he had preached fared no better. "Oh, minister," he enthused, "that grand sermon of yours was far too short."

"If you had listened with your soul, you would have been quite as exhausted as I was," replied Mr Macrae.

But, sharp in retort though he was himself, he did not mind when he was given his change in his own coinage. Some exchanges between him and his neighbour, Ian Cameron, have been preserved.

"Ian," asked Mr Macrae on one occasion, "am I a good neighbour?"

"The fence between us is a better," riposted Ian.

Ian lived in a thatched house that had only one door. Once, in calling for his minister, he rang the front-door bell of the manse. "Ian," queried Mr Macrae, "why do you always come to the front door?"

"Because," said Ian, "it is by my front door that you always come to me!"

The two Johns understood each other well.

But a sharp tongue can sometimes inflict a wound where this was not intended, as Mr Macrae more than once discovered. But when this happened he was quick to make amends. Casting his eye one evening over the day's work done by a man whom he had hired to dig his glebe, he said, "Is that all you have done today?" The labourer confessed that it was. "Then," said John Macrae, "you are not worth your wages."

A look of disappointment came into the man's face and his eyes filled with tears. Promptly, Mr Macrae healed the wound, that unintentionally, he had inflicted. The man was there and then engaged for more permanent employment, as a sailor on the minister's yacht. The work suited him well, and he did well in it. Master and man lived thereafter in complete harmony.

There was widespread poverty in Lewis in those days. Poor relief, where available, was scanty, and, in any case, few would ask for it. Poor relief carried a stigma, and, besides, an industrious, self-respecting people were unwilling to accept something for nothing. This led to a great deal of concealed hardship which kindly men, like John Macrae, found difficult to relieve.

Calling one day on a godly man, Angus Graham, he found him partaking of a meal which consisted of bread and water. To Mr Macrae's sympathetic remark about the quality of his fare Angus replied that he had what the Lord promised; *"bread shall be given him; his waters shall be sure,"* (Isaiah 33: 16). With that, he had the Lord's blessing, and he was content. But when John Macrae returned to his manse and saw his own table amply stocked with a variety of good things, not a bite of it would he take until a good share of it had been sent to Angus.

Chapter Nine

THE CHURCH UNION QUESTION

Big Macrae's ministerial life covered a critical
period in Scottish Church History. An Evangelical
from the beginning, he had been an ardent
supporter of the leaders who had championed the
Church's cause when her spiritual independence
was at stake, and when Parliament rejected her
final plea he was one of those who signed the Deed
of Demission, severing themselves from the State
and from all the benefits of Establishment rather
than surrender the Church's freedom. His gifts as
a spokesman for the Free Church, as we have seen,
were early brought into requisition and he became
widely known as an effective exponent of the
principles of the Free Church of Scotland. But
John Macrae was no separatist, and when
suggestions for the re-uniting of Scotland's
fragmented Presbyterianism began to be made his
interest was aroused.

The splits in the Secession Church began to be
healed as early as 1820 when the New Licht
Burghers and the New Licht Anti-Burghers came
together to form the United Secession Church in
that year. This body and the Relief Church united
in 1847 to form the United Presbyterian Church.
In 1852 a majority of that part of the Secession
Church which had not entered the United
Presbyterian Church joined the Free Church.
Ecclesiastical reunion was in the air, and a

movement for union between the Free Church and the United Presbyterian Church was initiated in 1863, when Committees were appointed by both Churches to inquire as to the measure of agreement between them, both in doctrine and principle, with a view to ultimate union.

The Joint Committee began its work in high hopes. What could be more desirable than that the walls of Zion should be repaired? But as negotiations proceeded, optimism began to wane. It became evident that the United Presbyterian Church had abandoned the Establishment Principle — a Principle that was part of the Constitution of the Free Church and of her public witness. The motion for the setting up of the Joint Committee — from the Free Church side — had recognised the duty of aiming at the accomplishment of union "by all suitable means," but consistently with "a due regard to the principles of this Church."

It was at this point that deadlock was reached in the negotiations, and when a motion was carried in the Free Church General Assembly to the effect that the differences between the conferring Churches constituted no bar to union between them, some members of the Union Committee — prominent Evangelicals such as Dr James Begg, Dr William Nixon, Dr Julius Wood and Dr James Gibson — resigned on the ground that the motion which had been carried in the Assembly implied "an abandonment and subversion of an admittedly constitutional principle of the Free Church of Scotland."

In his eagerness for Church union, John Macrae showed a disposition to stretch a point in the matter of Church and State relations, and regretted the intransigency, as he saw it, of Dr James Begg and Dr William Nixon. He had not himself drifted towards the Voluntary position, but he distinguished between one form of Voluntaryism and another. "What I could wish to see," he wrote to the Rev. Donald Macmaster, "is a strong healthy breeze blowing on the heap of Voluntaryism in the country with the fan in Christ's hand separating between the wheat and the chaff. In the midst of the Voluntaries there is a goodly number of excellent people whom I call the Spiritual Voluntaries* — the wheat — and a mixture of noisy people, let us call them Political Voluntaries — the chaff — who are filling the country with a religion without vitality, a frothy profession, only defiling those whom it affects. A separation of this kind might well lead to a healthy union, strong in the truth and fitted to become the salt of Scotland." This interesting hypothesis revealed that while Mr Macrae appears to have detected a new and jarring note in Seceder evangelicalism, he had under-estimated its seriousness. After events proved that Drs Begg, Nixon, Kennedy and their anti-Union associates were the more accurate judges of the emerging ecclesiastical situation. John Macrae was off the earthly scene before the United Presbyterian Declaratory Act of 1879, and the Free Church

---

* "Voluntaries" was the term applied to the upholders of the principle of Voluntaryism in Church and State relations. They held that "the State, as the State, has nothing to do with religion", whereas the supporters of the Establishment Principle emphasised the State's duty to maintain a national recognition of religion.

Declaratory Act of 1892, disclosed what they were meant to conceal, namely, that the projected union could take place only on the basis of a mutilated Confession of Faith. It was to cost a relaxation of vital doctrine as well as a virtual abandonment of the Establishment Principle. The winnowing wind which Mr Macrae looked for as a pre-requisite to a "healthy union" did not eventuate. It was not his "Spiritual Voluntaries" but the "Political" ones who were foremost in the Union negotiations.

In the end Mr Macrae opposed the Union movement although on grounds of expediency rather than principle. The General Assembly of 1870 had instructed the presbyteries of the Church to consider "whether, apart from other considerations bearing upon the present movement, there is any objection in principle to the formation of an incorporating Union among the negotiating Churches on the footing or basis of the Westminster Confession of Faith as at present accepted by the said Churches." When the Presbytery of Lewis took up this remit, the Rev. G. L. Campbell, of Lochs, moved "that there has not been shown to exist such unity in principle between the negotiating Churches as would warrant incorporating union in the manner suggested by the Assembly's remit." This motion having been seconded, "it was moved by Mr Macrae, Carloway, that the Presbytery find that there is no bar in principle to an incorporating union among the negotiating Churches on the basis proposed in the Assembly remit, but that in view of the sad divisions on this subject existing among ourselves, it is not expedient to proceed further towards consummating the Union proposed."

The minute of Presbytery bears that Mr Macrae's motion secured the support of his seconder only.

In a letter to Dr Elder, who was Moderator of the 1870 Free Church General Assembly, he writes, "I do hope that even should a majority of Presbyteries vote for Union on the ground of principle, it will not be forced in the face of opposition so determined, so bitter, and so strong, even numerically. Such a course could easily be construed as a violation of the law of brotherly kindness."

Mr Macrae's attitude on the Union question lost to him the favour of some of his brethren who were otherwise minded. Perhaps another paragraph in his letter to Dr Elder makes clear why, for a time, he was prepared to make certain concessions if only "a healthy union, strong in the truth, and fitted to become the salt of Scotland" might be reached.

"What a pity," he writes, "that Protestants could not be brought to be of one mind, so that a fair fight might commence between the Papacy stripped of its secular power, on the one side, and an open Bible on the other. Then we are sure the sword of the Spirit would triumph over every error. It is not the war without, but the fightings within, that weaken and darken the interests of Protestantism."*

---

* It is possible to discern the influence of Mr Macrae's hero, Dr Thomas Chalmers, in this plea. Chalmers was much criticised for his support of Catholic Emancipation in 1829, and even suspected by some of the extremer Separatists of having pro-Roman Catholic leanings. Nothing could be wider

True words, these, expressing a lofty ideal and making perfectly clear that "Big Macrae's" brand of Unionism was very different from the reckless ecumenism of later times which, in the interests of a spurious unity, is ready to make major compromises in doctrine and confession, and which, instead of resisting the Roman Catholic Counter-Reformation movement, provides Romanism with the very facilities it desires for the regaining of its ascendancy in Scotland. Mr Macrae's unionism, on the contrary, was based on "an open Bible," and motivated by the desire that "the sword of the Spirit should triumph over every error."

But the unionism that produced the United Free Church in 1900 was of a very different character, and some of the more evangelical brethren who took part in it lived to regret their action and to express their disillusionment and disappointment.

Compromise in the Truth never marks the way to victory.

---

of the mark. Chalmers firmly believed that Romanism would never be overcome by the imposition and maintenance of oppressive disabilities upon the Roman Catholic population, and he pressed for emancipation, believing that in this change of attitude, a better climate for Reformed evangelism would be created. Intolerance and persecution would tend to confirm Romanists in the error of their system. But Chalmers was an ardent Protestant. The teaching of God's Word would be more effective in countering a resurgence of Roman Catholicism than would any of the political disabilities which had been imposed upon the Roman Catholic population. ". . . give me the circulation of the Bible," he said, "and with this mighty engine I will overthrow the tyranny of Antichrist and establish the fair and original form of Christianity on its ruins."

Chapter Ten

THE CLOSE OF THE DAY

After his year in Stornoway, following his resignation from the pastorate of Carloway, Mr Macrae resided for some months in Skye, thereafter returning to the scene of his former ministry on Clydeside. For a time he resided in Gourock, later in Kilmacolm, before taking up house in Greenock.

Developments in his old congregation saddened him. By that time the Rev. Murdoch Macaskill was minister. There was still a large congregation, but the unanimity of former days was gone. Mr MacAskill enjoyed a considerable reputation throughout Gaeldom as a preacher, although, in the judgment of many discerning hearers, his sermons were more showy than solid. A comment on the situation in a letter to the Rev. Donald Macmaster shows where Mr Macrae's sympathies lay. "Upon the whole," he writes, "matters do not appear to be prospering among them, and they have an opportunity of learning that abundance of sound, and volubility of speech is not all that is necessary for an effective ministry." In endeavouring to retain popularity with both the conservatives and the innovators in the congregation Mr MacAskill rather fell foul of them both. Archie Crawford, of Kames, who was a frequent and discerning hearer in the Free Gaelic Church, in later days, had warned Mr MacAskill what the result of his temporising would be. "You are trying," he said, "like a man in a circus, to ride two horses together, with a foot on each horse, and you won't manage it. The end of it all will be that you will fall between them."

The Argyllshire worthy's warning was prophetic. In the Declaratory Act controversy which agitated the Free Church in the early nineties of last century, Mr MacAskill assumed a vigorous lead among the Evangelicals who were defending the Constitution of the Church and contending for the Reformed position which her Confession pledged her to maintain. But in the closing stages of the pre-1900 Union discussions, he completely changed sides — won over by the resourceful Principal Robert Rainy. By then Mr MacAskill was minister of Dingwall Free Church. There he failed to muster a sufficient following to retain possession of Dr John Kennedy's fine old church and manse. Archie Crawford's prediction was fulfilled. He fell between his horses and was sorely hurt in the process. He did not long survive the Union of 1900. His former comrades in the Constitutional movement, who continued the Free Church of Scotland in her hour of crisis, did not hold his desertion against him, but were in frequent touch with him to the last. And after death had rendered his pulpit vacant, the Rev. Murdo Mackenzie, of the Free North Church, Inverness, — perhaps the best-known Constitutionalist in the Highland area — went to Dingwall to pay tribute to his fallen friend.

Mr MacAskill's ecclesiastical vagaries left a distinct impression on the Greenock Free Gaelic Church, although "Big Macrae", away back in

1876, could not have foreseen how disastrous they were to be. The fear that had prompted Macrae's action in the Presbytery of Lewis in 1870 when he had moved discontinuance of the negotiations for Union, lest they should bring disunity into the Free Church itself, was shown to have been well-grounded. By forcing through a merger which aimed at uniting two denominations, the Unionists split the Free Church of 1843 into three sections. The old Free Gaelic Church shared in the disaster. A Free Presbyterian section went out in 1893; the pro-Union party went out to form the United Free Gaelic Church; and the remanent Free Church adherents retained possession of the old Disruption building in Jamaica Street.

Mr Macrae's bond with his daughter, Jane (who became the wife of the Rev. Donald Macmaster), appears to have been specially strong. In his letters to her during his frequent absences from home, and after her marriage, there are passages which express concern for her health, and especially for her salvation. "My beloved child," he writes, "seek the Lord God of your parents."

Jane sought, and found, and it was to her that Mr Macrae wrote in the last letter that she received from him what must surely be regarded as one of the best definitions of grace ever penned. Here it is. "What a meaning there is in that word GRACE for such as I am. It contains everything necessary for the salvation of a sinner, leaping over mountains of aggravated rebellion, infinite in its absolute freeness. What I need is to realise this in its power and glory."

His last sermon, preached in great physical

weakness, but with wonderful unction, was based on the text, *"He shall feed His flock like a shepherd; He shall gather the lambs with His arm, and carry them in His bosom, and shall gently lead those that are with young,"* (Isaiah 40: 11). John Macrae was back to his early occupation as a shepherd; only now he was not the shepherd, but a member of the flock tended by the Good Shepherd Who laid down His life for the sheep, testifying to the unfailing goodness of Him Who, after leading him in green pastures and by quiet waters, guarding and protecting him by His staff and rod, covering his life with goodness and mercy, was now giving him an assured hope of dwelling in the house of the Lord for ever.

He passed to the realisation of that blessed hope on 9th October 1876, leaving to Greenock, as a last trust, the custody of all that was mortal of him "until the day break, and the shadows flee away." (Song 4: 6.)

SERMONS
AND
SERMON NOTES

Zech. 12 –10. 4th January 1872 Snizort

Promise
1 Revelation of God's purpose of Grace
2 Flows purely from divine benevolence
3 Free & unconditional
4 discriminating – house of David &
5 Revealed to faith – 5 Begets faith
Contents of this promise, Spirit of Grace
  1 Gracious in his nature
  2 Implants Grace in the hearts of believers
  3 Conveys & communicates supplies of Grace &
  of supplications –1 Begets life – 2 consciousness of
  spiritual wants – 3 Naturally turns to the source of
  all blessings 4 a praying soul – 5 Helped by Spirit

III Effects – 1 Looking to Jesus pierced – 2 Godly sorrow
  1 intense – 2 General – Individuals families

  1 Great duty on such a day as this – Prayer
  2 To believe that God will do what He hath said
  3 Pray for the poor Outcast Jews to whom
    this past promise was first given

Facsimile of a page of sermon notes from John Macrae's study Bible.

THE POWER OF THE BLOOD

Unto Him that loved us, and washed us from our sins in His own blood. —Rev. 1: 5.

1. *There is forgiving power in the Blood,* for "without the shedding of blood there is no remission." "Blessed is he whose transgression is forgiven, whose sin is covered." God said to the children of Israel, "And the blood shall be to you for a token upon the houses where ye are; and when I see the blood, I will pass over you, and the plague shall not be upon you to destroy you, when I smite the land of Egypt." It does not cry out for vengeance against sinners in this world, as the blood of Abel did. In my native district, in the dark times which preceded the introduction of the Gospel there, it used to be said that if a murder was committed, and the murderer was unknown, the first time that the guilty man, in the company of two or three other men, happened to pass in sight of the place where the body of his victim lay concealed, a spurt of the murdered man's blood would leap on to the face of the murderer, and thus he would be detected, convicted and condemned to death.

I do not say how much truth—if any—may be in that tradition, but it may be that God did such things in our land before the coming of the Gospel enlightenment and understanding. But, my fellow-sinners, this will I say, that though ye are guilty of the blood of Christ in rejecting and despising it, thus consenting to, and becoming implicated in His death as surely as were those Jews who crucified Him, staining their hands with His blood, and crying out, "His blood be on us, and on our children," His blood today offers forgiveness to you, and will never rise up against you to convict or condemn you, if you will believe in its pardoning power.

2. *It has Reconciling Power.* God is in Christ "reconciling a lost world to Himself, not imputing their trespasses unto them; and hath committed unto us the word of reconciliation." "And all things are of God, Who hath reconciled us to Himself by Jesus Christ, and hath given to us the ministry of reconciliation." God hath set Him forth "to be a propitiation through faith in His blood, to declare His righteousness for the remission of sins that are past through the forbearance of God."

3. *There is Cleansing Power in the Blood.* "The blood of Jesus Christ, His Son, cleanseth us from all sin." We must not, however, detach these words from the former part of the passage—"But if we walk in the light as He is in the light we have fellowship one with another; and the blood of Jesus Christ, His Son, cleanseth us from all sin." Whereas all other blood stains, and leaves unsightliness behind it, the blood of Christ cleanses from all stain, and makes the soul whiter than snow.

4. *There is Refreshing Power in the Blood,* comparable with the refreshing quality of spring water that refreshes the parched and thirsty traveller on his journey under a burning sun. When one is thirsty there is no drink more acceptable and refreshing than cold water. But the virtue present in the blood of Christ far exceeds that of spring water for it refreshes the poor soul parched under the condemnations of an accusing

conscience and the bearing of Divine displeasure which, like the burning rays of the sun, beat upon and shrivel up the soul. It refreshes the soul vexed with the temptations of Satan, and the persecutions of the world.

5. *There is Strengthening Power in the Blood.* "My flesh," said Christ, "is meat indeed, and My blood is drink indeed. He that eateth My flesh and drinketh My blood dwelleth in Me and I in him." There is a water-spring in the place where I was brought up, into which the strongest men used to put their hands to see who would longest endure the cold without flinching; and he who held out longest was reckoned the man of greatest strength. But soul, this water revives and strengthens you—the water of which Christ said to another, "If thou knewest the gift of God, and who it is that saith unto thee, give me to drink, thou wouldest have asked of Him, and He would have given thee living water." "The water that I shall give him," said Christ, "shall be in him a well of water springing up into everlasting life. The Lamb which is in the midst of the throne . . . shall lead them unto living fountains of waters"—this represents the power of the blood of Christ.

6. *There is Peace-Giving Power in the Blood.* "And He came and preached peace to you which were afar off, and to them that were nigh." It is the blood that speaks peace to the tossing, restless soul, without hope or prospect of rest—the soul guilty and lost till it hears Christ's voice saying, "Come unto Me all ye that labour and are heavy-laden, and I will give you rest"—or peace. "Learn of Me, for I am meek and lowly in heart, and ye shall find rest"—or peace—"unto your souls."

7. *There is Power of Attraction in the Blood of Christ.* It brings near. "In Christ Jesus ye who sometimes were far off are made nigh by the blood of Christ." "And I, if I be lifted up from the earth, will draw all men unto Me; this He said signifying what death He should die."

8. *There is Sanctifying Power in the Blood.* "For if the blood of bulls and of goats and the ashes of an heifer sprinkling the unclean sanctifieth to the purifying of the flesh, how much more shall the blood of Christ, Who through the eternal Spirit offered Himself without spot to God, purge your conscience from dead works to serve the living God?" "Who gave Himself for us that He might redeem us from all iniquity and purify" or sanctify "unto Himself a peculiar people zealous of good works."

9. There is another Power in the Blood—*the Power of Initiation.* The high priest could not enter the most holy place without blood, any more than one of us can enter into true nearness to God but by the blood of Christ. "Having, therefore, brethren, boldness to enter into the holiest by the blood of Jesus, by a new and living way, which He hath consecrated for us through the veil, that is to say, His flesh. . . ."

10. *There is a Power of Redemption,* or *purchase,* or *release, in the Blood* for those whom the law and justice held bound as prisoners, and whom nothing less than blood, even the blood of the God-man, the Lord Jesus Christ, was sufficient to set at liberty."

G

Thou art fairer than the children of men; grace is poured into Thy lips; therefore God hath blessed Thee for ever. Psalm 45: 2.

I. *Some respects in which Christ is the fairest.* In 1. *His Person;* God, Man, Mediator. 2. *His Work;* perfection in wisdom; faithfulness; perseverence in it. 3. *His Character;* humiliation, submission, obedience. 4. *His Manner towards the People;* e.g. the woman of Canaan; the woman of Samaria; Martha and Mary; the woman that was a sinner; the woman with the bloody flux; Peter, etc. 5. *He hath all beauty in Himself, and from Him all beauty is derived.*

Enoch excelled in close walking with God; Abraham in strong faith; Job in patience under sufferings; Moses in meekness amidst provocations; Joseph in moral purity; David in tenderness; John in love; Paul in knowledge; Peter in zeal; John the Baptist in self-denial.

Each of these excelled in one thing; Christ in all, and He communicated to each what each possessed. How great then must His beauty be!

II. *This beautifying grace was poured into His lips,* meaning the fulness of the grace given Him; meaning also that it was by His word He was to beautify His people. 1. By His Word He rebukes them. 2. Enlightens them. 3. Comforts them. 4. Opens their hearts. 5. Strengthens them. 6. Beautifies them.

III. *The Blessings that follow.* The prosperity of His undertaking. 1. He finished transgression. 2. Made reconciliation for iniquity. 3. Brought in everlasting righteousness. 4. Redeemed His people. 5. Spoke peace to the Gentiles.

IV. *Seasons when He manifested His beauty.* 1. Cana of Galilee (His first miracle). 2. Mount of Transfiguration. 3. His baptism. 4. In the conversion of His people.

V. *The effects of seeing His beauty.* 1. It makes a lasting impression. 2. It casts a veil over everything else. 3. It beautifies the person seeing it (Moses: 2 Cor. 3, 18).

Those who see it ought to declare it.

Carloway, 13th and 20th December 1868.

THE CAPTAIN OF THE HOST

And he said, Nay; but as captain of the host of the Lord am I now come—Joshua 5: 14.

Remarks on Joshua as a type of Christ.

I. *The Lord has a host.* 1. Gathered from among the rest—by the Word; by the Spirit; by Providence. 2. Made willing in a day of power to fight under Christ their Captain. 3. Joined to the Lord in perpetual Covenant. Jer. 50. 5; 4. Taught to live on the promises by faith. 5. An unpromising company of soldiers. Jer. 31. 8. 6. They are opposed by enemies, Numerous; Cunning; Unscrupulous; Having formidable power.

II. *It requires a rare person to undertake their leadership, but Christ is equal to the task.* 1. God proposed to bring them to glory. 2. He revealed this purpose in His promises. 3. God appointed

His own Son to this great work. 4. The Son consented to undertake it. In the fulness of time He appeared on the field. 5. He opened a way for mercy and for them. 6. He puts weapons (arms) in their hands wherewith to fight their enemies. 7. He goes before them, even at their head.

III. *His Qualifications:* A right; love and tenderness; power; sympathy; patience; resolution.

He stands by them, in obedience; sufferings; death; entering into glory. 1. Here is encouragement to the Lord's host. He is equal to His work. 2. He glories in it. 3. He conquers every enemy. 4. He never leaves them. 5. He pensions them all. 6. He will rejoice over them. 7. He triumphs over Satan.

IV. *To sinners and enemies:* 1. He is God's Gift. 2. He requires soldiers. 3. He refuseth none that cometh. 4. He takes vengeance on all that refuse.

Carloway, 31st October and 7th November 1869.

SOLOMON'S CHARIOT

King Solomon made himself a chariot of the wood of Lebanon. He made the pillars therof of silver, the bottom thereof of gold, the covering of it of purple, the midst thereof being paved with love for the daughters of Jerusalem. — Song of Solomon 3: 9, 10.

Mr Macrae's divisions and sub-divisions of his sermon are given as follows:—

I. *The Chariot*—the Covenant of grace.

II. *The Receiving into the Chariot*—the work of the Holy Spirit in the souls of God's people.

III. *The Character of the Chariot,* and its suitability—1. *The Maker of the Chariot*—King Solomon; that is, spiritually, King Christ. 2. *The Material of the Chariot*—Cedar from Lebanon, signifying durability. 3. *Pillars of Silver*—the Promises of the Covenant, (a) Comeliness; (b) Beauty; (c) Reliability; and (d) Preciousness.

IV. *The Bottom of the Chariot*—Gold, signifying value, stability, durability.

V. *The Midst of the Chariot*—Love.

VI. *The Covering of the Chariot*—Purple, signifying the sufferings of Christ.

Those who were favoured by being received into the chariot and transported to heaven are described as follows:—

1. We may make the first part of the text to read thus, "King Christ made Himself a chariot." Into this chariot, as it proceeds through this world to glory, Christ receives all His faint-hearted and destitute ones here below. The Holy Spirit, to speak with reverence, is Christ's charioteer. When Christ observes a broken-hearted wayfarer, He says to the Holy Spirit, "Stop, thou blessed Leader, here is one whom we must lift in; he is bewailing the hardness of his heart." 2. Passing on, Christ sees another person lamenting his darkness, and says, "Stop, that we may lift him in. 3. He next sees some one cast down with doubts as to whether he belongs to the family of God. Christ commands that he be taken in. 4. Proceeding, he descries one who mourns the weakness of his love to Christ, if he has any love at all. Christ says, "let us lift him in." 5. Passing on,

He sees another who is being tempted with doubts as to his having obtained a saving knowledge of Christ. Christ commands the chariot to be stopped to admit him. 6. He goes on till He next overtakes one lamenting the wickedness of his heart. Christ commands that he be taken in. 7. Going forward, He sees another sorely distressed with unbelief. He commands a halt in order to take him in. 8. Proceeding, He observes another person who sorely mourns, "The Lord has forsaken and forgotten me." Christ commands a halt that he be lifted in. 9. Proceeding onward, He sees another complaining, "My leanness, my leanness!" Christ says, "Stop, that we may lift him in." 10. Going on, He sees another lamenting over his backsliding, and commands, "Stop, that we may take him in." 11. Going on, He sees another who has grown weary of the world, and the world weary of him. Christ says, "Stop, that we may lift him in." 12. Proceeding, he observes another who mourns over his want of holiness. Christ says, "Stop, he needs to be lifted in." 13. Proceeding, He sees another who is under serious apprehension that he will never get to heaven. Christ commands, "Stop, that he may be lifted in."

MANIFOLD TEMPTATIONS

"Now for a season, if need be, ye are in heaviness through manifold temptations." I Peter 1: 6.

In the first place, they are in heaviness on account of their gloomy and depressing view of God's providence toward them in their tried and troubled state, while they reason that, if God cared for them as His own children, He would not leave them to despair. Again, spiritual depression causes heaviness; and these two things—dark providences and spiritual depression—are like gestation in a woman, which frequently produces lowness of spirits and slowness of gait. Thirdly, they are in heaviness from the backward condition of the cause of truth in the land, crying out, "O, God, plead Thine own cause. It is time for Thee to manifest Thy power." A fourth cause of heaviness is when injustice overcomes them and iniquity prevails against them. What is said of Gad, however, is also true of them; *"A troop shall overcome him; but he shall overcome at the last"*— Gen. 49: 19. A fifth reason for their heaviness is when they see some of their nearest earthly relations careless about the cause of God, and their souls without right or portion in Christ. This causes them deep distress and great heaviness, and they plead, as did the Apostle, *"My heart's desire and prayer to God is that they might be saved."* I can conceive the angels in glory sometimes wondering at God's dealings with His people in this world, and, as it were, asking God, the Creator, Who sends them forth to minister for them who shall be heirs of salvation—"We cannot understand why Thou should'st leave so many of Thine own people in such a miserable state in the world when many others who are not Thy people enjoy such happiness and comfort."

"O, My angels," I can imagine God replying. "You may wonder at such an arrangement. but rest assured that it is in the course of providence the best and most effective means of raising the hearts of My people on earth above earthly things and fixing them on things which are above, so that they may esteem the world as nothing, and set their affections more and more on the heavenly Kingdom and its everlasting felicity."

Poor and sorely tried though the Lord's people may be in the world, God has provided against their needs, and has a heartening word for them in their "manifold temptations". *"Hearken, my beloved brethren," writes James, "hath not God chosen the poor of this world, rich in faith, and heirs of the Kingdom which He hath promised to them that love Him?"*—James 2: 5. They need four things on the journey to heaven; 1. *They need the blood of Christ from day to day;* and I should hold that the greatest Christian is he who comes oftenest to the blood of Christ for cleansing. Though there were no sinful guilt resting on one's conscience to come to Christ with, yet that one sinful thought had found access to the soul of the true Christian, it would be enough to send him to the blood of Christ that he might have the defilement of that one thought purged from his conscience through the cleansing of the blood.

2. *They next require the Spirit of Christ to aid them in every duty.* Without Him they can do nothing, but they can do all things through Christ, or through the Spirit of Christ, strengthening them.

3. *They need, in the third place, the grace of God.* They would fain lay their hand to something pertaining to the cause of God, but they are often so impotent that they cannot do what they would desire to do. Sometimes, they have nothing but the shrunken and withered hand of unbelief to stretch

out as they call for "grace, grace, grace," for themselves, when they can do no more.

4. *They need the Word of God to be a lamp unto their feet and a light unto their path*. They will not presume to proceed with any undertaking without taking the Word of God as a light and a lamp to guide them. They constantly make the Word of God their chart to show them the right path, testing their every word, thought, and action, as well as their spiritual conditions by this true and certain standard, the measuring-rod of the infallible truth of God which abideth for ever.

I can picture the council of peace between the Father and the Son from eternity for the salvation of the lost race of men. God the Father was moved in His infinite love to the lost and ruined race of Adam, as foreseen by His omniscient eye. Then the attribute of justice came forward demanding how mercy could be extended to these sinful creatures except at the expense of justice, unless or until all the demands of Law and Justice were met. Then Holiness stood forth, showing forcefully and earnestly how impossible it was that the perfection of God's character could be presented, without spot or blemish, if His favour forever were extended to such unworthy creatures. Then the attribute of Divine Wisdom spoke, and said, "O Justice and Holiness, I am in full agreement with all that you have so rightly spoken, and for that very reason My unerring Wisdom has found a way whereby all My attributes shall be forever satisfied, and greatly exalted, when mercy is extended to those poor wretches.

Wisdom then named and marked out Christ, the second Person of the Trinity, as the one being suitable to, and capable of, the taking in hand and the working out of their salvation. This He did by taking to Himself their nature, yet free from sin, and suffering the penalty that they deserved for their sins.

The Love of God arose also and exclaimed "O, My Eternal Son, ever beloved of Me, art Thou willing to be made like one of them, and to do, and endure, all that is required on their behalf, so that My Mercy may flow out to them and deliver them from going down to the pit?"

To this, Christ gave His full and cordial assent, saying, *"I delight to do Thy will, O My God; yea, Thy law is within My heart."*

CAIN AND ABEL (Genesis 4)

A Contrast in Character

The two were brothers; had same instruction; same example. Yet in their moral character they differ essentially. Their employments were equally removed from any special temptation.

CAIN

I Had a form of religion; was not an atheist.
II Acknowledged God's supremacy.
III Observed the Sabbath.
IV Offered sacrifice. His religion would do if he were not a sinner.

He came short in that;

I He had no true sense of sin; no faith; no love.
II His religion did not improve his moral character.

II It was a hot-bed for the more malignant passion of his nature.

ABEL

I Believed God's testimony through the teaching of his parents.
II Mourned over the sinfulness of his depraved nature.
III Felt his need of the promised Saviour.
IV His heart was broken—his spirit contrite.
V He embraced Christ by faith and offered a blood sacrifice.
VI The first martyr; the first man to enter heaven.

To which of these types do you belong?

THE GOD WHO PARDONS

Who is a God like unto Thee, that pardoneth iniquity, and passeth by the transgression of the remnant of His heritage? He retaineth not His anger for ever, because He delighteth in mercy. He will turn again, He will have compassion upon us; He will subdue our iniquities; and Thou wilt cast all their sins into the depths of the sea.—Micah 7; 18, 19.

I. *Pardon of Sin*—Fundamental Blessing. 1. Originating in Divine goodness. 2. Founded on Redemption.

II. *The Nature of the Pardon. 1. Free. 2. Full. 3. Forever.*

III. *The Extent of It.* 1. Extends to guilt. 2. It changes a man's state and relation to God and

His law. It does not remove sin itself. This has been a snare to many. 3. It removes the curse. 4. It delivers from condemnation.

IV. *The Importance of It.* 1. It flows warm from Divine goodness. 2. Comes through the Mediatory work of Christ. 3. Opens up the way to every other blessing. 4. It is revealed only to Faith. 5. It is contrary to conscience. 6. To the law. 7. To reason. 8. It is communicated through union to Christ.

V. *Errors about It among Gospel hearers.* 1. The senseless. 2. Those that have some thoughts about general mercy, but are not in earnest. 3. Those labouring under sore conviction, and betake them to duties, not to Christ. 4. Those whose sins land them in despair as Judas.

Learn. 1. The exceeding evil of sin. 2. The goodness of God in sending His Son to open up a way for this mercy. 3. The exceeding love of Christ. 4. The obligation of the pardoned.

Seek union to Christ Who is exalted to give this royal gift. Never rest till your sins are pardoned.

Greenock, 14th November 1875.

THE SECURITY OF THE CHURCH

Upon this rock I will build My Church; and the gates of hell shall not prevail against it. —Matt. 16: 18.

Peter's confession of faith—"Thou art the Christ."

God's work—Building up a Church.

I. *The Foundation of it*—the Person of

Christ. 1. God's Son by eternal generation. 2. Possessed of the same essence and attributes as the Father. 3. His only Son. 4. His Beloved Son. 5. His obedient Son. 6. Clothed in human nature. 7. Anointed of the Holy Spirit. 8. Sent forth as Saviour of the world. 9. He is thus the Church's foundation.

II. *His Work now is building the Church on this foundation*. 1. He received the Spirit. 2. Instituted the means of grace. 3. Raised up men to be under-builders. 4. Their work (*a*) to show the foundation; (*b*) to call on all men to rest on this foundation; (*c*) The Holy Ghost is given them for their work.

Sinners are convinced 1. Of Sin. 2. Of Righteousness. 3. Of Judgment. They are supernaturally enlightened; taught of God. They discover that if they are not on this foundation, they perish.

III. *The Opposition to this Work*—the gates of hell. 1. Beelzebub. 2. Hosts of demons. 3. The unconverted. 4. Formalists. 5. Hypocrites. 6. Unconverted ministers. 7. False brethren.

Subjects for self-examination.

Marks of believers. 1. Appreciate Christ. 2. Distinguish between conscience and their own wild feelings. 3. Not led by selfish and wordly motives. 4. Seek Christ's glory in God's way.

Kilmuir, 1st June 1873.

THE TRANSFIGURED CHRIST

This is My beloved Son in Whom I am well pleased; hear ye him.—Matt. 17: 5.

1. The death of Christ is the grand theme of

Scripture. 2. Nothing in earth or heaven creates so intense interest as this. 3. Jesus was on the eve of death—the death of the cross. 4. Two men were sent from heaven to confer with Him—Moses and Elias. 5. A voice from heaven testified to Him in the hearing of three witnesses 6. These were His credentials as an ambassador from heaven to earth; from God to men; to transact with men for God, and to transact with God for men who were rebels.

I. *Let us first see how Jesus is the Beloved Son of God.* 1. He is God's Son by eternal generation—thus the Son of His love. 2. He is perfectly like the Father — "The brightness of His glory," etc. 3. He is ever-dutiful to His Father in the most difficult of duties (involving persecution; the Garden; the Cross; death.

II. *The Duty of all to whom the Gospel is preached.* To hear Him. 1. Reverently. 2 Implicitly. 3. Alone.

III. *Some of the things He says.* That 1. He came into the world to save sinners. 2. He that believeth and is baptised shall be saved. 3. He that believeth shall not be damned. 4. He is able to save to the uttermost. 5. "Come unto Me . . ye shall find rest," etc.

Turn not away from Him. Remember that *you* need salvation.

DECISION

Now therefore fear the Lord, and serve Him in sincerity and in truth. . . ." Joshua 24: 14-24.

Man's creatureship. He must have a master to serve.

His nobility; his services are solicited by the Lord, and by Satan.

His choice is awfully important; for it he is responsible.

I. *The Service Satan Prescribes.* 1. Disobedience to all God's commands. 2. Diverse lusts (Titus 3: 3). 3. Envy. 4. Malice. 5. Following old companions.

II. *The Nature of this service.* 1. Low and degraded. 2. Guilty. 3. Destructive. 4. Slavish. 5. Draws down God's displeasure (the Antedeluvians; Sodom; Jews; Individuals. The consequences of Satan's service are seen in these).

III. *The Service the Lord Requires.* 1. Intelligent. 2. Willing. 3. Performed in the Name and strength of Christ. 4. Single-eyed. 5. Self-denying. 6. With sorrow for shortcomings. 7. At the expense of grace. 8. Persevering.

IV. *The Nature of this Service.* 1. Honourable. 2. Well-rewarded. 3. Performed by Free-men. 4. Reasonable. 5. Sanctifying. 6. It is the way to answer the chief end of man. 7. Promotive of true happiness.

V. *The Choosing of the Service.* You must do it. And *now*.

The difficulties of the service. 1. Human weakness. 2. Corruption. 3. Temptations. 4. Love of ease. 5. Love of the world. 6. Carnal pleasures. 7. Mistaken views of liberty. 8. Hatred of holiness. 9. Following others.

VI. *What Kind of Master Christ is.* 1. Kind. 2. Of long-experience. 3. Sympathetic. 4. Strong to help. 5. He pleads for them. 6. He will be with them at their work. 7. He employs sinful men. 8.

By such He triumphs. 9. Through them He obtains much glory.

VII. *The Resolution of Joshua.* 1. He tried it long. 2. Met many difficulties. 3. Was but a man. 4. Yet made up his mind. 5. Stood to it. 6. Died in service.

VIII. *Pre-requisites to this Service.* 1. Born again. 2. Enlightened. 3. New heart. 4. New will. 5. Love to the Master. 6. Hatred to sin. 7. Grace reigning in the heart.

Carloway, 10th March 1867.

ADVICE TO THE AFFLICTED

And call upon Me in the day of trouble; I will deliver thee, and thou shalt glorify Me.—Psalm 50; 15.

I. *All our race are liable to trouble. "Man is born unto trouble as the sparks fly upward."* Job 5. 7. Psalm 32. Cain, Judas—No peace for the wicked.

The Lord's people also have their full share. Christ says so: *"In the world ye shall have tribulation."* John 16; 33. The Apostles were told so: *"We must through much tribulation enter into the Kingdom of God."* Acts 14: 22. *"These are they which came out of great tribulation."* Rev. 7: 14.

Consider Job; Joseph; Moses; Jeremiah.

Seasons of trouble. 1. Conviction of sin. 2. Unfruitfulness. 3. Corruption. 4. Temptation. 5. Death and judgment.

II. *The Exhortation,* "Call on Me." Implying, 1. Renunciation of all other objects of hope. 2. Knowledge of the Throne of Grace. 3. Faith in Him seated on it. 4. Spreading one's case before Him. All this is consistent with the use of lawful means. 5. Waiting at the posts of His door.

III. *The Answer Promised.* 1. Either immediate deliverance, or 2. Grace to endure it. 3. This is usually done by the Word.

IV. *The End of it All.* "Thou shalt glorify Me." In 1. Acknowledgment of God. 2. Thanks offered. 3. A more tender walk. 4. Being more watchful. 5. Having more confidence. 6. More patience.

SONS OF GOD

But as many as received Him, to them gave He power to become the sons of God, even to them that believe on His name. —John 1: 12.

The theme is Adoption.

I. *Who were adopted?* They were 1. Aliens. 2. Slaves. 3. Under the law. 4. Under wrath. 5. Dead.

II. *The Change Effected in them.* They were 1. Redeemed. 2. Quickened. 3. Called. 4. Made willing. They 1. Approved of salvation by Christ. 2. Embraced Christ. 3. Were justified. 4. Received into God's family — adopted.

III. *Their Privileges.* 1. Dignity. 2. New name. 3. Spirit of His Son. 4. Liberty in their Father's service. 5. Access to God. 6. Title to inheritance.

113

H

7. Fatherly care and protection. 8. Ministry of angels, sanctified affliction.

IV. *The Nature of their Adoption.* 1. Costly. 2. Honourable. 3. Free. 4. Perpetual.

V. *The Character of their Father.* 1. Compassionate. 2. Rich. 3. Wise. 4. Almighty.

Note the misery of the outcasts. They have, 1. No peace. 2. No purity. 3. No title. 4. Rank poverty. 5. A cloud of wrath settled over them. 6. Death reigns in them. 7. The axe of Justice will soon cut them down.

Carloway, 8th December 1867.

ALL FOR GOOD

And we know that all things work together for good to them that love God, to them who are the called according to His purpose. —Roms. 8: 28.

I. *Who they are.* "Them that love God, who are the called according to His purpose." 1. The law is written in their hearts. 2. They have a new nature. 3. Love what the law requires of them. 4. They understood, and believed God's love to sinners. 5. They saw the excellency and glory of this love. 6. They felt a drawing in it of their hearts to Him. 7. They hate themselves because of sin in them. 8. They thirst for holiness. 9. Love God's house and service. 10. They live on the promise.

II. *They are called effectually.* 1. From death to life. 2. From darkness to light. 3. From sin to holiness. 4. From enmity to love.

III. *The "all things" that work together for their good.* 1. Trials of life. 2. Temptations of Satan. 3. Dark Providences. 4. Delay of Promises. 5. Poverty of spirit. 6. Folly of professed friends. 7. Infirmities of old age. 8. Emptyings from vessel to vessel.

IV. *The "Good" here spoken of.* 1. They are made partakers of God's holiness. 2. He hurries them home. 3. Looses them from the world. 4. Proves what is in their hearts. 5. Prepares them for possession.

God's perfections are engaged to secure their good.

Christ's offices are executed for this purpose.

The Spirit's work also has this end in view.

THE ALL-INCLUSIVE GIFT

He that spared not His own Son, but delivered Him up for us all, how shall He not with Him also freely give us all things?—Roms. 8: 32.

These words imply that all mankind were in a perishing state; that none could be saved but by the substituting of the Son of God for them.

The question then was, shall He be given, or shall all perish forever?

The Father decided the question as in the text. Faint likeness to Abraham.

I. *To what was He given up and not spared?* 1. Poverty and its attendant evils. 2. The enmity of Men. 3. Temptations of Satan and his hosts. 4. Curse of the Law as a Covenant. 5. Sword of Divine Justice. 6. Bruised between wrath of God and His own deity. 7. Desertion which is the essence of death. 8. Death for a time. 9. His body to the grave.

II. *Things they need which He will certainly give them.* 1. Pardon. 2. Brokenness of heart. 3. Strength for duty. 4. Fruit unto God. 5. Renewed supplies of grace, of life from the Head. 6. Tenderness of conscience. 7. Love to Christ. 8. Spirit of adoption. 9. Liberty to call God Father. 10. They would honour God in the world.

III. *How He gives all things.* 1. In union to Christ by faith. 2. Freely; no price, no merit.

The Character of those to whom this belongs. *

1. They appreciate Christ. 2. Renounce self-righteousness. 3. They love the law of the Lord. 4. Give up old ways and companions. 5. Delight in the Sabbath. 6. They have done with lying. 7. They have given up the world as their portion.

At the Lord's Table.

1. The Elder Brother is at the head of it. 2. His poor friends are the guests. 3. His broken body and shed blood the matter of the Feast. 4. He is rich. 5. Hospitable. 6. Loving. 7. Humble. 8. Gospel Promises are the golden vessels. 9. Acknowledge your obligation to Him; He brought me in. 10. Give Him your heart love; He gave you so much.

Glenshiel Communion, July 1868.

---

* *The theme of the sermon was continued in the fencing of the Table, and in the address at the Communion Table.*

THE POWER OF THE CROSS

For the preaching of the Cross is to them that perish foolishness; but unto us which are saved it is the power of God.—I Cor. 1. 18.

I. *The preaching of the Cross, what is it?* It is to proclaim reconciliation to God through Christ's death on the Cross, implying that men are transgressors of God's law. 2. That God is offended. 3. That His Justice must be avenged. 4. That nothing can satisfy Justice but blood and death as was threatened. Implying also that Jesus Christ voluntarily stood between the elect and this vengeance. He took 1. Their nature. 2. Their law room. 3. Became answerable for their sins. 4. He suffered the punishment due to them. 5. Died for them — poured out His soul to expiate their sin.

Having satisfied the avenging Justice of God by His blood. 1. He was released from death. 2. Rose again. 3. Was exalted to the right hand. 4. Invested with power to dispense the blessings of the covenant which He satisfied by His death. 5. Now proclaims peace through the preaching of the Cross.

II. *The preaching of the Cross is to invite sinners to look to the Cross for salvation, certifying that those who come and look shall freely receive.* 1. Pardon. 2. Peace. 3. Life. 4. Liberty. 5. Faith. 6. Repentance. 7. Love. 8. Adoption. 9. Holiness. 10. Heaven as their home. 11. God as their portion.

III. *The preaching of the Cross ensures for believers abundance of grace.* 1. For trials. 2. For duties. 3. For warfare. 4. For the wilderness journey. 5. For the last enemy—death.

IV. *The preaching of the Cross has power.* 1. To convict sinners. 2. To convert. 3. To hold on. 4. To Perfect sanctification. 5. To glorify.

Carloway, 12th June 1870.

SPIRITUAL DISCERNMENT

But the natural man receiveth not the things of the Spirit of God; for they are foolishness unto him, neither can he know them, because they are spiritually discerned. —I Cor. 2: 14.

I. *Things that natural men receive and know.* 1. The Being of God. 2. The Power of God. 3. The Holiness of God. 4. The Justice of God.

II. *Things that natural men cannot receive or know.* 1. The Sovereignty of God. 2. The Incarnation of Christ. 3. The Reign of Grace. 4. The Love of God to sinners in Christ. 5. The Death of Christ in the room of sinners. 6. The Mercifulness of God's nature. 7. The Life of Faith 8. The Victory of Christ by suffering. 9. The supernatural revealed by the Gospel.

III. *The reasons for this.* 1. Spiritual blindness. 2. Perversion of mind.

IV. *How the Natural Man is changed.* He is—1. Made a new creature. 2. Adapted to the Covenant of Grace. 3. His mind is totally changed. 4. Enlightened. 5. His heart is softened. 6. His will is renewed. 7. His conscience is sprinkled with the blood.

God is seen in a new light as 1. Amiable. 2. Excellent. 3. Glorious. 4. To enjoy Him is the highest happiness. 5. To serve Him is the highest delight. 6. To be conformed to Him is the ruling desire.

V. *The things of the Spirit are* — 1. Revealed. 2. Offered. 3. Necessary. 4. Suitable. 5. Those that receive them shall certainly be happy.

Those that receive them not shall be miserable. For them there is, 1. No pardon. 2. No mercy. 3. No salvation. 4. No change of character. 5. No life. 6. No fellowship with the Father or His Son. 7. Heaven shall be shut. 8. Hope extinguished. 9. Despair shall become active. 10. Hell a reality.

Carloway, 9th October 1870.

HEIRS OF GOD

Wherefore thou art no more a servant, but a son; and if a son, then an heir of God through Christ. —Gal. 4: 7.

I. *Unconverted men are all servants in the light of Scripture.* 1. Servants of Sin (Roms. 6: 16) 2. Of Satan—a god, and a prince. Such masters are like the taskmasters of Egypt. Their bondage is 3. Spiritual. 4. Guilty, vile. 5. Destructive. 6. Provoking to God. 7. It ripens for eternal punishment.

II. *How are these slaves made free?* 1. They are redeemed from the curse of the law. 2. The price of their redemption is the substitutionary death of Christ. 3. He puts into them the Spirit of His Son. 4. Faith. 5. Love. 6. They have liberty to serve Christ. 7. Are adopted into His family. 8. Constituted heirs of an inheritance of which God is the sum.

III. *They are made* 1. Heirs of Promise (Hebs. 6: 17 and 11: 9). 2. Of Righteousness (see Hebs. 11: 7). 3. Of Salvation (Hebs. 1: 14). 4. Of a Kingdom (James 2: 5). 5. Of the grace of life (1 Peter 3: 7). 6. Of God. 7. Of all things.

IV. *Properties of the Inheritance.* 1. Incorruptible. 2. Sure. 3. Satisfying. 4. Everlasting. The Spirit is the earnest of it: they are preparing for it.

V. *See the wonderful goodness of God.* 1. He needed them not. 2. What they were—abject slaves. 3. The costliness of Redemption. 4. The high dignity of their privileges. 5. The wonderful love of God. 6. Believers are the excellent of the earth. 7. God is both rich and liberal.

The misery of slavery; slaves are cast out. But there are overtures of mercy to such.

DELIVERANCE AND TRANSLATION

Giving thanks unto the Father, which hath made us meet to be partakers of the inheritance of the saints in light; Who hath delivered us from the power of darkness, and hath translated us into the Kingdom of His dear Son.—Col. 1: 12, 13.

I. *The Deliverance.* Who is the deliverer?—The Father.

From What Darkness? 1. Sin. 2. Error. 3. Misery. 4. Death.

II. *The Power, wielded by Satan.* 1. Misrepresents God. 2. False hope. 3. Insensibility. 4. Despises authority of God in law and gospel. 5.

Love of sin and darkness. 6. The example of others.

III. *How the Father delivers.* 1. He purposed it. 2. Sent His Son. 3. Accepted a ransom. 4. Gave Him the Spirit—to enlighten them—to give a true sense of sin—to create in them a desire for liberty—to convince them of total inability—to cast out the Prince of this world—to make them willing to accept deliverance and to come out of prison.

IV. *Their Translation into the Kingdom of Grace.* Privileges. 1. They are under the reign of grace. 2. All their wants are supplied. 3. They are clothed in perfect righteousness. 4. Guided in the right way. 5. He heals all their diseases. 6. Sanctifies them wholly. 7. Defends them from all enemies. 8. Educates them. 9. Chastises them. 10. Gives them eternal life.

V. *Their Meetness for Heaven.* 1. They come to Christ for life. 2. Are perfectly justified at once. 3. Sanctified progressively. 4. This capacitates them to enjoy God. 5. No more sin. 6. A pure nature. 7. Temptations cease. 7. No fear of death. 8. God is all in all. 9. They are light, as God is light. 10. Darkness fleeth away.

Carloway, 12th September 1869.

THE NEW JERUSALEM

Blessed are they that do His commandments, that they may have right to the tree of life, and may enter in through the gates into the city.—Rev. 22: 14.

I. *The Residence of the Saints*—is compared

to a city—New Jerusalem, suggesting—1. Beauty. 2. Security. 3. Unity. 4. Presence of the Lord. 5. Holy laws. 6. Fellowship with the Lord and with one another. 7. Immortality. 8. Complete happiness.

II. *The Tree of Life*. It is there with its twelve manner of monthly fruits. It symbolises Christ Whose blood is effectual. 1. To remove guilt. 2. To pacify conscience. 3. To establish liberty. 4. To excite an appetite for holy food. 5. To restore and perpetuate peace. 6. To revive from fainting.

His death is sufficient to: 1. Appease God. 2. Satisfy His justice. 3. Meet all the demands of the broken law. 4. Satisfy the Covenant of Grace with all its blessings. 5. The tree is in the midst of Paradise—on either side of the river for perfect convenience. 6. Sufficient for all. 7. The Holy Spirit is there with His divine influences without restraint.

III. *The Way to the City*—"doing His commandments." 1. Faith complying with the Gospel call; believing the Truth; accepting Christ. 2. Love—the fulfilling of the Law. 3. The spiritual mind meditating upon His commandments. 4. The new heart approving of them all as holy, just and good. 5. The will choosing them.

They have a right to Christ the Tree of Life, not of merit, but of meetness.

Those that shall be without. Dogs — Sorcerers — unclean — murderers — idolaters — liars.

Carloway, 23rd October 1870.

Blessed be the God and Father of our Lord Jesus Christ, which, according to His abundant mercy hath begotten us again unto a lively hope by the resurrection of Jesus Christ from the dead.

To an inheritance incorruptible, and undefiled, and that fadeth not away, reserved in heaven for you, Who are kept by the power of God through faith unto salvation ready to be revealed in the last time.—I Peter 1: 3-5.

I. *The Author of Salvation.* The God and Father of our Lord. He 1. Devised it. 2. Ordained it. 3. Judged it. 4. Accepted it. 5. Performs its conditions.

II. *The Source of Salvation.* 1. Abundant mercy. 2. Love. 3. Grace. 4. Goodness—words which are but modifications of the same general idea, the infinite perfection of God's nature.

III. *The Two Parts of Salvation brought out in these words.* 1. Regeneration. 2. Inheritance.

Regeneration is: 1. The work of the Spirit. 2. The sinner is passive in it. 3. It involves a change of nature. 4. A new relation to God. 5. Sins pardoned. 6. The person accepted. 7. The adoption of sons.

The Provision of an Inheritance. It is: 1. Incorruptible. 2. Undefiled. 3. Unfading. 4. Reserved. 5. In heaven.

They are *kept* for it—means faith unto salvation. Perseverance is a precious Bible doctrine. With Paul all believers bless God for salvation—its hopes and its privileges.

IV. *The Lively Hope.* 1. Its Warrant—the word of promise. 2. Its Foundation—Resurrection of Christ. 3. Its Nature—lively, operative. 4. Its Object—an inheritance.

Greenock, 30th May 1875.

Knox Press (Edinburgh) Publications

SCOTTISH THEOLOGY IN RELATION TO CHURCH HISTORY SINCE THE REFORMATION
by Principal John Macleod, D.D.
350 pages   £1.65

One of the most useful books ever published. Surveys the whole field of Scottish Theology, and passes judgment upon all from the viewpoint of orthodoxy.—*K. A. Macrae.*

HERITAGE OF OUR FATHERS
by Professor G. N. M. Collins, B.A., B.D.
171 pages
£1.50 (hardback); £1 (paperback)

An up-to-date survey of Scottish Church History, with special reference to the Free Church of Scotland.

"Professor Collins' readable and instructive work should be in the hands of all who desire to know the course of events in Scotland from the Reformation to the present day." — *The English Churchman.*

JEREMIAH: THE MAN AND HIS MESSAGE
by Alexander Stewart, D.D.
276 pages   £1.25

Exegetical and Expository Studies in the Prophecy of Jeremiah by one of the most outstanding preachers in the Scottish Church in this century.

BYPATHS OF HIGHLAND CHURCH HISTORY
by Principal John Macleod, D.D.
Edited by
Professor G. N. M. Collins, B.A., B.D.
162 pages   42p

An interesting compendium of Highland Church History popularly written.

SANDY AND ANN
by Irene Stewart, M.A.
28 pages   15p

A delightful booklet for children from the pen of a gifted Christian teacher. Profusely illustrated.

"Attractively produced . . . the book would make a suitable gift item for children, ages about 8 to 12 years." — Dr J G. Vos in *The Blue Banner*.

THE SHORTER CATECHISM
WITH LAWSON'S NOTES — New Edition
64 pages   8p

GOD'S LIGHT ON MAN'S DESTINY
by Professor R. A. Finlayson, M.A.
79 pages   22p

A helpful study of Reformed eschatology viewed in the light of Biblical Revelation.

GAELIC POEMS OF JOHN MORRISON:
the Harris Blacksmith
350 pages   £1.50

A spiritual classic.

ON THE INDIAN TRAIL IN
PARAGUAY AND BRAZIL
by Rev. Harry Whittington
194 pages   77p

A thrilling story of pioneer missionary work.

THE PRACTICE OF THE
FREE CHURCH OF SCOTLAND
52½p

THE WESTMINSTER
CONFESSION OF FAITH
AND FREE CHURCH STANDARDS
22½p

THE KNOX PRESS (SCOTLAND)
15 NORTH BANK STREET
EDINBURGH